THE HUNTING DOG
TRAINING BIBLE

ANDY HOWELL

ABOUT THE AUTHOR

Hi there! Before we get into the nitty-gritty details of e-collar training, I thought we would start this e-book out through a basic introduction. My name is Andy Howell. I am a dog trainer, an animal lover, and an all-around adventurist. I have been working with animals since I was a young kid, and I have been e-collar training for over fifteen years now. Currently, I reside on the East Coast and work, diligently, with a close group of pups every month through bootcamp training. Yet, more than that, I also work with different dog owners and trainers in facilitating proper behavioral methods, obedience, and e-collar training. But, more than this small description of whom I am, I thought I would go ahead and tell you a little bit more about myself and my path with dogs.

Growing up, life was pretty boring for me, except for when I had the opportunity to go on the road with my family. My family travelled around the United States a lot when I was a kid, so I never really had a "permanent" home. During my family's travels, I used to always visit animal shelters when we would make pit stops in different cities. This is how my journey with dogs *truly* began. First a passionate kid and then an aspiring advocate, my relationship with animals really took off when I was visiting a shelter in Northern California when I was seventeen years old. My family decided to spend the summer in Northern California after making a pit stop at an old friend's. I decided to spend my free days volunteering at an animal shelter and surprisingly, I met the love of my life. He was a scared little dog that sat in the back cage of the shelter, and his name was Cannon. Cannon was only around five years old, had a roughed-up spirit, and was more than a little bit wounded. Our relationship expanded exponentially when I was able to convince the Head Manager at the shelter to let me work with Cannon in the yard. Everyone thought Cannon was mean and unable to be trained, which meant euthanasia was on his tail. But, with the approval of the Head Manager, I worked every day with Cannon. We had some rough times, but Cannon prevailed. His anger and aggressive tendencies dissipated, his personality cheered up, and soon enough, Cannon found a new home right before he was about to be put down. This experience showed me that anything is possible with our dogs because they have a potential that is endless. Training isn't always about obedience. Sometimes, it's about giving your dog what they need and teaching them that it's okay to behave rightfully, and also that it's okay to mess up along the way while receiving help from their loving owners.

Since this summer long ago, my path has been solidified, and dogs have been "it" for me. Now, I hope to inspire and assist anyone and everyone with training because I believe dogs and humans should both should be happy, healthy, and living a great life through togetherness.

INTRODUCTION

For those with energetic pets that enjoy being outdoors, training your dog to assist you with hunting can be a great way to burn off some of that additional energy. It is a useful skill that can be taught by utilizing proper techniques that have proven successful over the last several decades. Training a hunting dog can be one of the most challenging, yet most rewarding, tasks for a pet owner. Over time, a dog will naturally be able to pick up on your cues. Not only is having a hunting dog practical, but it's a great way to get your dog the exercise it needs. When training your dog, you will need to remember that hunting takes multiple skills. All the tasks won't be as simple as sitting down, staying, and fetching, but your dog will need those fundamental skills in order to be a well-rounded dog that is suitable for all of your hunting needs.

I recommend that you get your dog when it is a puppy so that you and your dog can bond from the very beginning. A dog is going to trust you more if you are able to establish that great bond. Aside from spending time with your puppy, you are also going to need to make sure that it is socialized properly. A lot of behavioral issues can arise when a dog is kept isolated from other people and other animals. For the best results during training, you are going to want to make sure that your dog is experienced in many different situations. Depending on the type of hunting you are going to be doing, you will need to do the proper research to know which commands are going to be the best ones to teach. All of these components are necessary before you begin the training process.

Remember, it is within your dog's nature to want to please you. As long as you keep the activities fun, you should have no problem teaching your dog all of the necessary steps and commands that it takes to be a great hunting dog. When you come up with a great reward system, the tasks will become fun like a game rather than hard work. A dog that is being rewarded for doing the right thing will continue to do so in the future. Make sure that you remember to keep your bond with your dog strong because, at the end of the day, it is up to the bond that you share to get you to your end goal.

If you want more great information, sign up for my newsletter for weekly dog training tips!- https://bit.ly/2XM9gi2

1

CHOOSING YOUR PUPPY

Picking a puppy that comes from a line of dogs that are already in the field makes the most sense. This is the logic that gun dog trainer Clyde Vetter uses. He believes that dogs who come from parents that have done this before will have it in them to do the same. In his experience, clients that bring him puppies to train that fit the description have an easier time catching on to the training process. This is one way to ensure that you are making the smartest decision for both yourself and your dog. He also suggests that you get a solid idea of temperament before selecting your puppy. Although, this can change over time, having a good initial temperament is very important.

Even though field scores earned by the parents will not necessarily accurately reflect the puppy's performance capability, Vetter believes that it still helps to know this information. In fact, he recommends only selecting a puppy from a breeder or seller that knows your intended training purpose. Those with dogs born to hunting parents will likely raise the puppies the same way, already making them accustomed to the lifestyle. When this is the case, that means there will be even less work for you to do as you begin the training process.

What to Do First

Your first step in selecting a hunting dog begins before you decide to go out looking for puppies. It is important that you have a clear purpose in mind before selecting the type of dog that you want to train. Are you going to be bird hunting? Deer hunting? Will you be using a gun? Will you opt for a bow? All of these factors are going to have to be taken into consideration in order to know what dog breed will best suit your needs. These are the 10 most popular dog breeds that are used for hunting:

Labrador Retriever: One of the most common dog breeds in the world, Labs are great companions and hunting dogs, alike. Duck hunting is something that they especially excel in. They have ample amounts of energy, as well as a coat that is suitable for most climates. It protects them because it is thick, but it is also cooling when the dog is in motion. A Lab is also keen on being in the water, which is important for duck hunting purposes. Often going to great lengths to please their owners, Labs will make it a mission to retrieve your kill for you. They range from about 50-80lbs, the perfect size for a hunting companion.

American Foxhound: Just as the name suggests, this breed is great for helping catch small game. As they have evolved over time, the Foxhound has been used for deer hunting, as well. This is a very athletic breed that excels while hunting. On average, they weigh around 60-70lbs. A lot of hunters enjoy keeping an American Foxhound because they are relatively low-maintenance. They are also pretty even-tempered—perfect for when they are off duty and keeping you company at home. Because of their incredible speed, they can be trained to retrieve just about any animal that you are able to hunt. Don't let the name fool you, they are a very versatile breed.

Beagle: This is a smaller breed to select, but the Beagle is a mighty contender. Standing just over 1-foot tall most of the time, this dog is a great choice for any small game hunter. They are very eager and persistent and not easily distracted by outside events. When in the moment, your Beagle is going to only have one purpose in mind, and that is to help you with the hunt. Another plus is the endless amount of energy that the dog seems to have. Because they have such great noses, it is possible for them to succeed both in packs and alone. Easygoing in nature, with the proper training, a Beagle can learn how to use their keen sense of smell to assist you thoroughly.

German Short-Haired Pointer: This beautiful breed makes for a great hunting dog. It is a diverse type that ranges anywhere from 45-75lbs in size, easy enough to bring along with you on the hunt. Because they are pointers, they are best known for their speed and agility. As you can imagine, these are key traits to look for when selecting the best hunting dog. While they are great at retrieving the kill, they have an additional skill—Pointers will show you where the game is located. Following this direction, you will have a much more successful hunt because of your furry friend. The most common type of hunter that selects this breed is the bird hunter. Pointers were bred to detect birds, so keeping them on their natural abilities will likely end up with the most positive result.

Bloodhound: Known for their keen sense of smell, utilizing a Bloodhound as your hunting companion has its obvious advantages. If you are looking for a dog that will easily be able to pick up scents, look no further. They love to track down prey for you, feeling accomplished when they are able to help you with the task. It is essential to properly train a Bloodhound if you want an effective hunting dog. Since they weigh around 110lbs, it can be a challenge if their behavior isn't monitored from an early age. Because they are so curious in nature, their noses might eventually end up leading them astray. Once you get them up to speed, they are able to trek through nearly any terrain because of their solid build.

Weimaraner: A beautiful dog breed, hunters like to choose Weimaraners because of their agility. A lighter build (most often weigh around 50-90lbs), they are able to run incredibly fast and clear jumps of many different heights. These are great skills if you plan on making a Weimaraner your bird hunting dog. But even if you hunt other game, you won't be disappointed with this breed. They have a calm temperament and will be able to remain as such when you are out in the field. This is essential for a hunting dog because distractions can often lead to barking and other disruptive issues that will scare the animals away. When you have a Weimaraner by your side, you will feel secure in knowing that your dog is there for the same purpose that you are.

Bluetick Coonhound: This breed was meant to hunt raccoons; it is what they are naturally born to do. Notably stealthy and keen on listening, the Bluetick Coonhound has the endurance to withstand most any terrain for any period of time. This is a dog that will be able to keep up with you no matter what the season is. They thrive at night, working well in the dark because the raccoon is a nocturnal animal by nature. With an extremely strong prey drive, all it takes is a little bit of guidance for your Coonhound to become a great hunting dog. At the largest, they tend to become is around 80lbs, which makes for the perfect medium-sized breed to bring along with you on your hunts.

Irish Setter: Known mainly for having beautiful coats, Irish Setters are not one-trick ponies. If you are a turkey hunter, this is a breed that you will definitely want to consider. The setter is known for speed, and this is important when you are working with any kind of fowl. With elegance and grace, they are able to easily retrieve your kill for you. Despite being able to assist with hunts that involve larger animals, the Irish Setter typically only grows to become around 75lbs. This is a smaller breed when compared to some of the other popular hunting dog choices. It is easy to travel with an Irish Setter because of its smaller stature and calm demeanor.

Plott Hound: When it comes to big game hunting, a Plott Hound is going to be able to get the job done. These dogs are able to keep up with hunts that involve animals as large as bears. This is a strong and fierce breed, perfectly capable of becoming a hunting companion. Their endurance and versatility will work in your favor as you trek over any terrain, even when it becomes treacherous. Judging by what they are capable of out in the field, you would think that this is a rather large breed. However, these dogs only grow to become around 40-60lbs in size. It is the perfect example of never judging a book by its cover; Plott Hounds are tough little animals that work very hard when they are given tasks.

Brittany: Popular among bird hunters, Brittanys are a more compact breed of dog. Weighing in at a mere 35lbs, it is by far one of the smallest breed choices when it comes to hunting dogs. Despite their appearance, Brittanys are actually very fast and athletic. This is a breed that has a lot of additional energy that must be released daily. Training the dog to hunt is a perfect way to allow that energy to be expressed in a helpful way. Being incredibly versatile is another benefit to selecting a Brittany—they are able to assist you with small game hunting as well as retrieving waterfowl.

Thinking about your different options when it comes to dog breeds, you will probably realize that there are a lot of factors to consider. Determine what you would like to hunt and when you would like to go hunting. This should help you narrow down the search. Remember, getting a dog as a puppy will provide you with a unique bonding experience. Not only will you get to properly train your dog with habits that will be beneficial in the hunt, but you will also get to spend time with it as a companion. A happy dog is normally one that is not only a hunting dog, but part of the family as well. Make a checklist of the most important traits that you can think of in order to help you stay focused on what will end up being the perfect breed for you.

Finding the Right One

Once you have narrowed down your search to the breed that is going to suit you most, you can start contacting breeders or shelters. While it is great to obtain any animal from a shelter, you aren't always going to be able to find the specific breed that you are looking for. This becomes especially true when you are seeking a puppy that comes from a line of hunting dogs. Doing some simple internet research can lead you to breeders in your area for the specific type of dog that you are looking for. Try to make several appointments to see several different puppies before you make your decision. Remember, you are going to need to get along with the dog on a working level and a personal level. This is something that you are going to have to feel out upon meeting each one.

Make sure that the breeders you select are ones that

value the overall health of the dogs. Your breeder should maintain a level of care before you adopt the pup, ensuring that it has its proper shots and preventatives. The key to a long, healthy life is an owner that makes vet visits a priority. When you first arrive, take a look at how many other puppies are in the litter. How do they interact with one another? Are there any that stand out to you, behaviorally? You will want to make note of any pups that are shy and skittish. A hunting dog needs to be used to several different environments, loud noises included. A fearless puppy is going to make a much better candidate than a shy one.

The personal bond that you first create is going to matter a lot during the training process. You have to make sure that your dog trusts you from the very beginning, or else it will not do what you are asking of it. Try to play with the puppies for a good amount of time before making your final selection. It would even be wise to come back more than once to see if the dog responds to you in the same way as it did upon your first meeting. This will also give you a more accurate representation of temperament.

2

CHOOSING A GROWN HUNTING DOG

Caring for a puppy takes a lot of work; this is no secret. When Rick Thompson decided that he wanted to get a hunting dog, he was actually fairly new to the pastime. He and his wife had retired long ago, seeing children off to college and turning bedrooms into offices. With a bad knee, Rick knew that he would not have the ability to run around the home after a puppy. It just wasn't a realistic option. Instead, he decided to get a grown dog that was able to do the job. Even though he did not have the dog as a puppy, Duke and Rick formed an unmistakable bond that just could not be beat.

He held the same standards when getting his dog that one would when selecting a puppy. Ancestry can help you in a lot of ways, giving you clues as to what the dog has naturally within. Rick selected Duke after a visit to a local breeder. He was calm, yet curious. Upon walking into the room, Duke walked up to him and immediately sniffed his hand. He continued to sniff around the room, assessing the situation with Rick the newcomer. In that moment, Rick knew that this was a future hunting dog. Curious by nature with a keen sense of smell, Duke went on to become the best duck hunting partner anyone could ask for.

Physical Ailments

When seeking a dog that is no longer a puppy, you will need to pay close attention to its physical health. Dogs that are 7+ are already considered to be a part of the "Senior" category. This normally isn't a problem as long as the dog has been mostly healthy for its life. When you first take a look at a dog, you can tell a lot about its health by the way that its nose and coat look. You will want to make sure that the nose is healthy, not cracked or dry. A wet nose is a sign of hydration and health. The coat should be shiny and well-maintained. If you notice a dull tinge, that might be an indication that there are some health problems.

Take a look at the dog's eyes. Are they clear and bright or glazed over? Having good eyesight is a huge part of being a successful hunting dog. He will need to keep his eye out for predators and also be able to spot and retrieve your kill for you. A lot of older dogs are prone to cataracts or glaucoma, so it is important to pay attention to the eyes. Are his ears clean? It is easy for a dog to contract ear mites (they look like black specs of dirt inside the ear). Pay attention to any itching or head tilting when you first meet the dog. While ear mites are relatively easy to get rid of, you will want to know if this particular dog is prone to them or not.

Asking the breeder about the dog's joints is also essential. A hunting dog must be able to move in an agile fashion, covering many different terrains. With bad hips and knees, your dog is going to have a short career in hunting. Getting the most up-to-date information on this from the breeder paired with giving the dog a joint supplement is going to be the best way to keep your dog healthy enough to hunt. When you first get your dog, it also isn't a bad idea to take him to the vet for a checkup straight away. Even if it does not look like any physical ailments exist, there could be some underlying problems going on.

Diet and Exercise

A balanced diet is important to your dog, especially you mean for it to engage in lots of physical activity. Find out what the dog has grown up eating. When you get a dog that is already grown, it is probably best to keep him on his original diet. A change in food might upset the dog's stomach or make him anxious. Bringing him into a new home is already going to be a huge change. If you do decide that you want to put him on a different diet, you must slowly substitute the old food with the new. For example, you can incorporate ¼ cup of the new food one week, ½ after that, and ¾ as the last transition until the dog is ready to fully switch over.

Ask if the dog is used to eating table food. This can be a tough habit to break if you do not intend on feeding him scraps in your home. A lot of training issues can arise when the dog is used to getting this type of food. You withholding it will likely result in begging or an outburst in behavior. While this doesn't have to be a deal-breaker, it is something that you should probably know ahead of time so that you are prepared. Allowing your dog to have a piece of meat every few days is a healthy alternative to feeding him scraps. You can cook plain chicken breast or a steak if you do decide that you want to give him that extra boost of protein. Stay away from the processed or artificial foods.

Learn about his prior history with exercise. Was he kept in a pen or allowed to roam free in a yard? There are two main ways that a grown dog will act after being kept in a confined area for long periods of time—he will either be very calm when let out, or he will be wild and bouncing with energy. This depends a lot on the breed and temperament of the dog that you choose. Just keep in mind these two outcomes, though. Find out if the dog has ever been swimming before and how he feels about water. Of course, this could become crucial to the dog being able to serve as your hunting dog.

Know that training a hunting dog is going to require a lot of running, so you are going to want to make sure that you have enough space to do so. A yard for your dog to run around in and to feel safe in is important. The yard should feel like his domain; it will give him the chance to learn that he needs to protect you and your family. If a dog has not been used to running his whole life, you are going to have to ease into it. Play with him as much as possible using toys that encourage his natural ability to catch and retrieve.

Cognitive Ability

While you can't necessarily ask the breeder how intelligent the dog is, you can put this to the test yourself. Bring a puzzle toy along if the breeder allows you to. Make note of how the dog reacts to it. A good hunting dog is going to show interest in toys and treats that you offer him. If he does not express the desire to play with it, then you might want to select a different dog. A hunting dog is a dog that must actively engage at all times. See how quick he is able to figure out the toy and take a look at what he does in order to reach the end result. Those with great cognitive ability usually act like puppies even when they are grown. They show a sense of wonder and desire to complete the task.

A neurological problem that a lot of older dogs can encounter is seizures. Make sure that you discuss this with the breeder, finding out if the dog has ever had one. Even if they have only occurred at a young age, this could lead to problems in the dog's future. There isn't always a clear cut reason for why dogs have seizures. Unfortunately, it can often be something that just occurs as the dog becomes older. When getting any dog as a grown adult rather than as a puppy, you will need to make sure that you are prepared for any future ailments that might start to show up.

To keep a grown dog mentally healthy, he is going to need constant stimulation. This doesn't mean that he needs to be hunting 24/7, but rather given the opportunity to exercise his brain whenever possible. Keep toys around him so that he has the option to play as frequently as he would like. Take him to many places with you, showing him many different environments and settings. A social dog is one that has the ability to feel okay with new situations. Take him out to the fields that you intend on hunting during the off-season. This will get him used to the area for when you are actually ready to go on a hunt.

Temperament

Much like selecting a puppy, paying attention to the temperament of a grown dog is even more essential. Temperament is something that generally cannot be changed. In younger dogs, the behavior can be curbed or altered based on environmental factors or situations. A dog that is already grown will likely be very settled into his temperament. If you meet him and he is not very friendly, you are not going to be very likely to crack the shell. What you see is what you get when it comes to mature dogs. This is why the first meeting is a very important deciding factor. If you notice that the dog is unruly, or even unhappy, then this is probably not going to be the best choice for a hunting dog.

The dog you choose should be friendly and sociable to many different people. While he can maintain a fierce loyalty to you, he should not be afraid of or mean to others. Ask the breeder about how his temperament has evolved over the last few years. You will also want to gather information on how he is around other dogs and animals. If he is a dog that acts aggressively toward other animals, you are going to have a hard time when you bring him out into the field. Even if you get a dog that becomes easily distracted, this could mean that he will run off at the first sight of another animal that he sees. You want him to be interested in what is going on without the need to stray from you until you give him the proper command.

Find out about any prior training that the dog has. A dog with an even temperament will likely retain information pretty well. Since you have the advantage of the dog being older, selecting one that already has some training will only make your job easier. This is not to say that you can't teach an old dog new tricks, though. A common misconception, older dogs are actually very trainable. They respond well to commands because they are able to be more focused than a puppy sometimes is. You can take advantage of this concentration and temperament by setting up a nice reward system for your dog.

If you want more great information, sign up for my newsletter for weekly dog training tips!- https://bit.ly/2XM9gi2

3
———

TRAINING BASICS

Getting to know your puppy is one of the most fun parts about training. You get to begin working together so that your pup will be prepared for the tasks that he will encounter in the field. A young man once began training his Bloodhound to help him retrieve ducks during hunts. The pair quickly formed a bond, working each day after the man got home from work. He created several different games that the puppy was responsive to, making the training feel like fun rather than a chore. They both enjoyed this so much, and the puppy was getting more and more comfortable responding to the various commands that were given.

As the puppy got old enough to hunt, the young man decided that it was time to put all of this training to the test. He was nervous that, when it came down to it, the pup might freeze up in the moment. Being great at listening to commands in the backyard is one thing but being able to spring into action during the actual hunt is another. As the man shot down his first duck, it went spiraling down into an open field. His Bloodhound looked up longingly, pausing and waiting for a command. "Get it!" he shouted, and watched the dog take off. Within a few minutes, he was back at his owner's side, placing the duck at his feet. In this moment, the young man knew that all of his training had paid off.

1-2 Months

DURING THESE FIRST FEW MONTHS, you should be doing dog training basics such as the commands for sit, stay, come, and lay down. This is also when your dog should be potty trained. Having a strong foundation is going to help you when you begin the more complex commands that revolve around the hunt. Get your dog used to a training system, one that you set up and stick to from the beginning. Think about how you would like to reward your dog and when you would like to do so. Training treats come in handy during this time because associating good behavior with food is a great way to win almost any dog over.

IF YOU'D LIKE, you can get a training clicker. This is a button that you can press to make a firm clicking noise. A lot of people like to use them with their dogs because it provides a unique sound that the dog can associate with good behavior. It can come in handy for training sessions where you might not have a treat or reward to provide. Clicking the device and praising your dog is another valid way to show him that he is doing exactly what you want him to. If you get him used to the clicker at a young age, you can continue using it well into his training as a mature dog.

You SHOULD ALLOW your dog to know the difference between a play session and a training session. During playtime, you can use a softer tone and allow your dog the freedom to roam as he wishes. To differentiate a training session, put on a voice is that slightly deeper and a tone that is firm. You don't want to scare the pup, but you do want to establish that during this time, he must obey you. Keeping the two voices exclusive will help your dog form an association between casual and serious time.

IT IS okay to keep the training light during this time because the puppy is still going to be developing his temperament. This is a good time to observe his behavior, taking note on how he responds to various cues and rewards. Even though your puppy is still incredibly young, he will be very eager to learn new things. Allow him to become socialized; invite new people over. Take him places in the car with you and bring him to dog-friendly establishments. Getting your dog used to all different types of people will allow him to be comfortable in most any environment.

BEFORE THE PUP COMES HOME, you should also invest in a quality crate. This crate is not only going to serve as a safe space for your dog, but also a way to enhance training. Allow your dog to know that going into the crate means that it is time to settle down or to travel. This is also a useful technique for teaching your dog how to use the bathroom outdoors. As soon as he is let out of the crate, he should also be let outside. Make sure that you utilize the crate for all purposes, not just travel to the vet, for example. This will cause the opposite response in your dog, actually making him fearful of being crated.

2-3 MONTHS

THE SAME BASIC training principles are going to apply during this stage. As the puppy begins to grow, he will be figuring out his body and his abilities. Encourage him to run as much as possible, giving him the chance to explore. When you do all of this, make sure that your dog is properly vaccinated and protected from the elements. If you live in a wooded area, you need to watch out for ticks and other insects that tend to gravitate toward dogs. As you are creating commands for your dog, keep them basic. A puppy is going to be much more responsive to 1-word commands at first than entire sentences.

KEEP GIVING your dog toys to play with, introducing new ones regularly. This will keep him engaged and interested. If you have any children or younger members of the family, absolutely allow your dog to socialize with them. Children have the energy that is comparable to that of a puppy, so they can often be a great match. When your pup is allowed to socialize with children, he will know how to act playful, yet gentle. As you invite guests over to your home, allow your puppy to meet everybody.

. . .

THIS IS ALSO the perfect time to let your dog meet other dogs. Socialization with people is just as important as socialization with other animals. Allow your dog to meet several different size dogs of several different breeds. Short trips to the park would be a great way to get that social time in when your dog is still young. Make sure to monitor his behavior and step in if he is getting too roughed up. Extended play that is too rough can often change your dog's demeanor, making him harder to train.

3-6 Months

ONE OF THE most basic first hunting-related commands you can teach is "Whoa!" This is a good one for pointers, especially. It indicates that your dog should stop moving and stay exactly as they are. This is an important skill to have because if your dog is moving around too much during the hunt, he might scare off animals. When the pup sees another animal, it is probably within his nature to get excited. You will want to train your dog to keep this excitement, but to reel it in so that you have the chance to take your shot. This command is made to do exactly that. Nearly all hunting dogs are first taught this command as a basic.

YOU CAN TRAIN this one by utilizing a suitcase leash and a board. This type of leash is made to secure the dog around the haunches, giving you a good amount of control. Bring your dog out into an open area, preferably a yard. Fasten him into the leash and set up your board. This type of "whoa board" measures around 2X3' and sits about an inch above the ground. When you pull up on the leash, your dog will be lifted in a similar fashion to a suitcase, coming completely up off of the ground. Place him onto the board and tell him, "whoa." This is supposed to establish the point that the dog should not move.

BY PLACING the dog in a defined space, you are asserting your dominance while simultaneously giving him guideline for what you want him to do. The message that you want to get across is that you do not want the dog to leave his post. At first, your dog will probably stay on the board for a few seconds at a time -- that's okay! Make sure that you praise your dog and give proper rewards for the amount of time that he does stay on. You can incorporate this skill in your training routine as it is very simple. The best way to form a good habit is by doing something on a regular basis.

THIS IS an appropriate time to introduce your pup to a bird for the first time. By allowing him to see one early on, this could ignite his desire to bring your kills to you. Make sure that your dog knows the command for "stay." In the field, this can be changed to "hup." When you are showing him the bird, you need to make sure that he will sniff it and then back off once you give him the command. If there is an opportunity, let your pup get into some shallow water. This is going to be an important aspect of being a hunting dog, so you will want to make sure that he is --comfortable with swimming and getting wet.

6-12 MONTHS

. . .

IF YOU WANT to utilize an electric training collar, now would be the appropriate time. This is a collar that sends out small bursts of electric current in order to let the dog know that he needs to stop what he is doing. While this isn't a method that every hunter utilizes, you can do this for your dog if you feel that he needs some extra guidance. You will have a remote that you can use to send out shockwaves when you need to. Many people believe that this is a cruel method of training, but you can use your best judgment when it comes to the techniques that you would like to utilize.

ALLOW YOUR PUPPY TO be around when you shoot your gun. He needs to be able to get used to the loud noises without getting frightened or excited. Take him shooting with you frequently and let him sniff the gun so that he knows what it is. Of course, you want him to be wary of running in front of gunfire but calm enough to know what is happening so that he doesn't run off in the moment. Get together with a group of other hunters if you can, exposing your dog to the sound of several rounds of gunfire. The more exposure that he has, the more likely he will be able to remain focused when you are out in the field.

AT THIS POINT in the training, your puppy should have obedience down. He should stay put until you give him the command to do otherwise, showing enthusiasm when you let him know that it is time to spring into action. The thing to remember is that dogs are able to pick up on many different things, especially when they are so young. Habits that you form early on will serve as a foundation for the future of any training that you do. Anything that you are able to do with your pup at home is going to help him out when he is in the field. One of the biggest things is just spending enough time with him and getting to know his behaviors.

4

TRAINING IN THE FIELD

Once your dog has the basics of training down, you get to bring him with you out in the field. An extensive amount of additional training happens during this time because the dog is able to gather live examples. The next part of this guide will break down the steps that you need to know in order to continue your training regimen.

Fetching the Kill

Most people believe that teaching a dog to fetch your kill revolves around the skill of fetching a rubber ball—this isn't the same thing. Because the ball is only a toy, the dog knows that this is a fun game. When retrieving something that was once living, your dog is going to have a different demeanor at first. Sometimes, even the most obedient dogs will hesitate at your first command to fetch something that is dead. Animals sense and perceive death very strongly. Because you pup has never had the opportunity to do this before, he might actually be confused.

When you are doing field training, it is important to

make the setting as diverse as possible. You should include a lake or pond if there is one nearby. Some hunters think that easing into field training is the best approach, but that is actually a myth. Your dog will know all of the essential skills at this point, so allow him a realistic training session. When you do select your location that includes the body of water, the only thing you want to watch out for is the current. Don't settle in a place where the current is too strong, or your dog might not be able to swim against it.

The things that you will need to bring along are a mock duck, anchor, and rope. If you cannot access a decoy, then anything that floats will suffice for the training. You just need to make sure that it can fit in your dog's mouth easily. Your rope should be about 15-25ft in length. Bright colors work best in this instance, something that your dog can follow easily. The only requirement for the anchor is that is has a space for the rope to get pulled through. With these simple tools, you can create the perfect mock setup for your dog.

Scent is important during this stage of training. Your dog must be able to identify and be used to the scent. Rub the decoy with some raw meat in order to simulate a realistic scent. Of course, you must only rub the meat on the decoy within 24 hours of your training session; you don't want your dog to become sick. After this, you simply tie the rope through the anchor and then tie the other end around the decoy. When you get to the location, drop the anchor close to shore. Give the decoy your best throw, slinging it deeper into the body of water. During this part, your dog should be sitting beside you obediently and waiting for the next command.

One of the secrets to encouraging your dog to swim to

the decoy involves you getting in the water yourself. This part is tricky because you don't want the dog to just swim to you. If you do want to utilize this method, make sure that you only swim near the toy and not directly to it. The dog should be able to figure out the rest. By seeing you get into the water, he will realize that this is something that he should be doing too. Training revolves around your initial bond of trust. This is why all of that prior bonding is so essential leading up to this moment. Whether you get into the water or prefer to stay dry and use a command, let the dog get close to the decoy before bobbing it up and down. This will entice him to fetch it and create some excitement.

As you complete this exercise more and more, you can actually have the decoy dive under the water in order to give your dog more of a challenge. Wounded ducks will often do this. As soon as you feel that your dog has the decoy, you can drop the rope near you. He should be happily swimming toward you with the kill. Once he returns, reward him with plenty of praise and some treats. This positive reinforcement will let your dog know that he did exactly what you wanted him to. Repeat this exercise until your dog seems like he is tired out.

Recognizing a Live Scent

Sometimes, your hunt might involve coming up on birds that are on the ground rather than in the air or water. This next exercise will help your dog know what to do when he realizes that there are live birds nearby. Training for this is important because you know that you must be very quiet in order not to spook the birds. One wrong move, and they will scatter. You can start this one off with a decoy, too. Before you go out into the field, spray your decoy with some live scent. Let it fully dry before you begin using it. You can actually let your dog play with the scented decoy at home for a few weeks beforehand. This is going to establish a purpose for him. Give him some short play sessions with the decoy before you take it out into the field.

The next step is to take your dog out into a large, open field. Bring the decoy along, tossing it far away for your dog to fetch. During this exercise, your dog will clearly be able to see you throwing the decoy. Because he will have had time to play with it at home, he should be very eager to fetch it and then bring it right back to you. Make sure that you are providing rewards and praise for every successful fetch. This will show your dog that now he is performing a duty instead of simply playing with a toy. You can do this for a long while, letting him get very familiar with the decoy.

As you do this exercise over time, start to throw the decoy further and further away. Your goal is to challenge your dog a little bit more with each training session. At this point, you should come up with a command word that can be used in order to tell your dog to fetch. It can be something like "seek" or "hunt." Make sure that it is only something that you would use out in the field so your dog knows that it is different from ordinary fetching. Your dog will soon realize the association with the new command and the action that you are expecting from him. He should be able to master this quickly.

This exercise will get your dog ready for the real deal. When you take him out on a hunt, you will be able to use these commands with him to get close to your prey. Combined with your dog's ability to sit and stay put, you should have no problem with the transition from decoy to live animals. If you feel that your dog is ready, you can allow him to get the bird for you. This is an advanced step, but your dog will be a very quick learner. Dogs love the stimulation of the hunt; it gives them a purpose while also feeling excited.

Staying in the Pocket

As you trek though the field, it is important that your dog stays facing the same direction that you face. This will keep him focused and ready to spring into action at any moment. You must train him to stay in the "pocket." This is a space that ranges from 10 o'clock to 2 o'clock. For example, if you are facing south, you will want your dog to also face south and within the pocket. This pocket is a great way to train your dog because it does allow a little bit of flexibility. Dogs are naturally curious, and it would be nearly impossible to bring one into a hunting setting, only to stay perfectly still. You want your dog feeling alert and ready to move at the drop of a single command.

Your dog likely isn't going to find more prey behind you than he will ahead of you. Once you begin walking, anything that is behind you is likely already disturbed or aware of your presence. You will want to make the front area your focal point. Ensuring that your dog stays within the pocket isn't very hard to do. Take your dog for a walk on a 20-foot leash. Allow him a clear path that he can see easily. Let him know that he is allowed to roam ahead of you and explore. Make sure that once he exits the pocket, you clap your hands in order to quickly get him attention and to get him back on track. Point your hand ahead of you and continue walking him. You can tug on the leash slightly to let him know that it is time to start moving again.

Depending on how old your dog is, this might take a little while to master. That is okay though. Just remain patient and willing to work with him on it. As he gets used to training to hunt in the pocket, you can utilize a whistle to help give him commands. The whistle can be added after the clap and point. You can blow on the whistle to replace the tug on the leash. This will allow your hands to be kept free as you walk. Think about this skill in a realistic way -- of course, it would be nice if your hunting dog could master the art of staying exactly in the pocket, but that isn't going to always be the case. Different terrain will often lead him outside of the pocket. But if it makes sense to hold off on correcting him, you can use your best judgment.

Detrimental Practices

While the focus should be on doing everything the best that you can for your hunting dog, you should also be aware of things that will ruin his training. These are some of the ways that hunters commonly incorrectly raise their dogs that lead to disobedience or distrust out in the field:

- Raising the Dog in An Outdoor Pen: Since hunting dogs are going to be spending a lot of time out in the field, it is a common misconception that you should raise them to be outdoor dogs. This used to be true, several decades ago when kids used to spend hours at a time outside with their pets. Today, things are different. Bottom line is that the dog should be where the people of the household are. Growing up in a pen is an isolating and lonely experience. Allow the dog to come inside, if possible. This will get him used to living with the family and becoming a true member of the household. When your dog is inside, you also naturally communicate with him more. As you know, this is an essential skill for when you begin his hunting training.
- Don't Repeat Too Much: When you are teaching

your dog new commands, it is likely that you are going to have to try them more than once before he picks up on them. There should never be a point where you are repeating yourself up to 4-5 times. If your dog does not respond on the 1st command, it is not because he didn't hear you. Dogs can pick and choose what they would like to react to, just as people do. Maybe the environment doesn't allow him to feel safe or maybe he is just feeling stubborn in general. Constant repetition is not going to get the dog to change his mind. To trigger a response, you need to remember to assert your dominance. This can be done by changing your stance or your tone of voice. Allow your dog to know that you are the one who is in charge, but don't be a bully about it.

- Avoid the Shouting: It can be frustrating when you are calling out commands, only to be met with no response from your pup. Your instinct might be to raise your voice, and before you know it, you are shouting. Not only is this unnecessary, but it is also a sure way to confuse your dog. He will probably become scared and think that the command is a punishment rather than something that you want him to do. Dogs are extremely sensitive to temperament. Much like the prior issue, this could be avoided by asserting your dominance or even providing more training. Remember, it is not that your dog does not hear you, but he might be putting on a stubborn act.

- Using Pleading: When your dog gets far enough

away from you, he will no longer be in arms reach. Trust has been discussed several times before, but in this case, you will need to utilize your own trust in your dog. Seeing him get farther away from you can be nerve-wracking, especially if it is early on in his hunting career. Never plead to him to come back your way. This is the type of tone that seems to inflect a question mark at the end of it. If you want your dog to come back, use the commands that you have taught in the same tone that you always use. Being consistent is probably one of the best training methods that you can utilize. If your dog notices a change in tone, he might think that you are trying to play a game or that you are not expecting him to act on his learned skills.

- Running Off Energy: A huge mistake that a lot of hunters make is getting the dog "worn out" before a hunt. The idea behind this theory is that, if you let the dog run around until he is tired, he will be more likely to obey you during the hunt. This practice is damaging for many reasons. For one, it teaches the dog that he only needs to obey you when he is tired. It also makes you at risk for over-working him. Hunting can be a huge workout that takes plenty of endurance. If you have zapped this from your dog before you even begin the hunt, you can't expect him to perform his best. The same can be said before you train your dog. He does not need to run around prior to any training sessions. Teaching a dog self-control is just as important as teaching a person the same thing.

- Too Many Marked Retrieves: A marked retrieve is when your dog can see the kill fall, and he knows its exact location before retrieving. While this is a convenient situation, do not hesitate to use your commands when the kill is a blind retrieve. The longer you hold off on this, the more likely your dog will be confused when it comes down to it. His sense of scent is what will lead him to the kill, and you must have faith in his ability to do so. Also, too many marked retrieves show your dog that he is on the hunt alone, not needing to rely on you for help. When it is a blind retrieve, he will have to listen to you and trust that you know where the kill is. Doing a mixture of retrieves will show your dog that he is capable of hunting while also showing him that he still needs to rely on you for guidance. This is the exact balance that you want to keep.

- Experimenting with Distractions: Imagine that you have been shooting your normal gun around your dog since you got him. He does not mind the noise and is still able to complete all of his tasks while out in the field. When you get a new gun, what is the proper way to introduce this? The main thing that you want to avoid is treating the situation like a temporary experiment. The dog is going to be able to sense this, and he also might not respond favorably to it. Instead of bringing your dog alongside you as you shoot for the first time, start by keeping him at a distance. Start at 150 yards away, allowing your dog to hear the noise first. It will work even better if you can get your dog to watch in the distance while another dog is beside you retrieving. This will make the situation very enticing. When it is time for him to be beside you, he should be feeling confident about the gun while also very eager to start hunting.

5

DEALING WITH A DIFFICULT DOG

I magine being out on a hunt, one that you have been looking forward to for weeks on end. The weather is clear and there are birds in abundance. Relying on your hunting dog to point you in the right direction, you give him a verbal command. Just as you have drilled over and over again, he shows you where you need to go. As you tell him to stay, he ignores this command and darts straight for a group of ducks, causing them to flee. You've missed the shot and the opportunity to achieve your goal. This was the reality for John Chavez. His hunting dog, Blue, had never acted this way before. Why did he act out in this moment? Why did he ignore the command to stay put?

This can happen to even the most obedient of dogs. If it seems like this is out of character, there is probably a valid reason behind it. Knowing your dog is just as important as your dog knowing you. Observing his behaviors will clue you in as to why he is feeling a certain way. If you have made any changes in your dog's home life, this could definitely trigger him to act out. Being at home should allow your dog to feel safe and stable. Maybe you have introduced another family member into the home, or even another pet. Any disruption of the usual routine could send your dog into a pattern of behavior that might seem out of character.

Determine the Cause

Before you go about punishing your dog, think about anything that is out of his control that has changed lately. Even if you can't think of anything right away, consider any other factors that might have disrupted his routine. Even leaving an hour earlier for work in the morning could be enough to impact your dog. Because you make up your dog's entire social life, you need to consider that small things might impact him in bigger ways than you realize. Do your best to make sure that you are doing everything on your end to keep your dog's environment stable. Coming up with a reason before you get to thinking about solutions will make things a lot easier for you both.

The next step is to set aside some time to work on this behavioral issue. Nothing is going to change unless you take the time to change it. Make sure that you get in some good one-on-one time with your dog in order to establish a new sense of routine. Observe how he behaves during the times when you aren't training or working him. This can also give you a sense of how he is feeling overall. If he starts to act out when you are simply playing together, this could be an indication that he needs more attention. If you find that he is behaving perfectly normally during this playtime, maybe he is finding the work that you are giving him to be boring. Either way, both of these issues can definitely be fixed.

Breaking Bad Habits

Dealing with discipline is something that becomes a part of being a dog owner. Even when you are not out hunting in the field, you need to make sure that your furry friend is acting right. If you let him get away with certain things at home, this is going to send him mixed messages that he is allowed to do these things all the time. The best tip when it comes to this is keeping a consistent set of rules in place. No matter if your dog is playing at home or running free out in the field, as long as you stick to your standards, you should have minimal behavior issues.

- Chewing: This is a very natural behavior for dogs to display, and it might even be acceptable during playtime. However, when you are out hunting, you need to make sure that your dog isn't going to become distracted by chewing on things. This could be an indication that your dog is stressed out or even bored. When you go on your hunt, you need to make them seem as exciting as possible for your dog. Give him plenty of praise and rewards when he completes a task for you. If you need to, let him perform additional tasks for you while you are waiting for animals to come along. Kong toys are great for getting chewing out of a dog's system. They are made of the most durable rubber and cannot easily be destroyed. Let him chew on his toy weekly and see if this makes any type of improvement on his behavior.

- Barking: An essential habit that must be controlled, nobody wants a hunting dog that is going to bark unexpectedly. Not only will this scare off animals, but it is also a big way for your dog to display his disregard toward your attempts to be dominant. If your dog frequently barks at you without your command, you probably need to reestablish this dominance between the two of you. Revert to some of the training exercises that you worked on in the very beginning of his hunting career. Going back to the basics serves as a nice refresher, and it also allows you to show your dog that you are the boss. When you are teaching him something with the power to reward him afterward, dominance will be put back into place.

- Digging: This is a very rewarding habit for dogs. It allows them to have fun while also feeling a sense of accomplishment. Of course, you don't want your dog to start digging holes around you while you are trying to hunt; this is just another form of distraction that can arise when boredom is being felt. Again, you must keep him engaged and focused on what he is supposed to be doing. You might need to work on training exercises that will allow your dog to solve some puzzles. Toys that release a treat after the puzzle is solved are great ways to engage your dog's brain. Work on this at home and you should see an improvement on his focus while you are out in the field.

- Begging: Even if your dog only displays this behavior every once in awhile, it can often get worse very quickly. A begging dog can be disruptive both inside the home and on the hunt. Begging usually stems from your dog wanting food that you are eating. If you throw him scraps from time to time, he is going to begin to expect them. This occasional treat will develop into a regular occurrence that is expected from now on. You don't want to open a pack of crackers while you are hunting, only to have your dog standing in front of you while whining. Try to limit the amount of table food that he receives. Only allow him to eat during designated feeding times and when he is getting praised for good behavior with a treat.

- Marking: When a dog marks his territory, this is his way of establishing boundaries. This is actually an indication that your pup has a lot of confidence, which can be a great thing. When it becomes a problem is when he starts to mark his scent inside of the house. As best as you can, interrupt your dog each time that you catch him attempting to mark indoors. A simple "no" will do the trick. Make sure that you lower your voice and change your tone so your dog knows that what he is doing is wrong. Once you cause him to feel ashamed and clean up all previous urine scents with an enzyme-based cleaner, this behavior should stop. You do not need to prolong the punishment because this will just create confusion. Ease up after you scold him, but make sure that he notices your brief change in demeanor. Dogs are great at picking up this type of body language, so it should not take too many tries before you notice the changes.

More Socialization

Sometimes, your dog will require a different type of change in the environment. Because boredom is a huge source for bad behavior, it might be best if you allow your dog some playtime with other dogs. You can do this in several different ways. If you have any friends or neighbors who have friendly dogs, invite them over so that they can have some playtime. If your dog is weird over his own space and territory, you can meet at a park or other public space so that neither one of them gets defensive. If you can find people who have other hunting dogs, that would be ideal. Utilizing the behaviors that other hunting dogs already have will almost be like a way to re-train your dog because he will be learning by example. A lot of people forget that hunting dogs have the same needs as ordinary house pets; they love to play. In fact, they might have even more energy than the average dog.

If you don't know anyone else that has dogs for your dog to play with, there are meetup groups that you can search for. There might even be some breed-specific options so that your dog can socialize with other dogs of the same breed. There are just some things that can only be learned from dog to dog, and that is why socialization is so important. Take a look at your local dog parks. If your dog is friendly enough, you can take him there. Dog parks are a great way to not only socialize your dog, but you can also meet other owners in the local area. The dog park also provides you with the option to get your dog used to being around other people. This aspect of socialization will be helpful for your dog's demeanor.

Combating Aggression

While hunting is a way for your dog to let out some of his natural pent-up aggression, you need to be careful that this does not show up in his daily behavior. Aggression can appear slowly over time, in the most unsuspecting ways. If you notice that your puppy likes to grab onto your child's shirt while they are running around in the yard, this is a behavior that must be monitored. The same can be said for other "domineering" habits that you notice your dog displaying. A little nipping at the ankles can be cute and even funny at first, but it can turn into a big problem as the dog matures if he is not told to stop this behavior. If the dog is still young, crate training might have to be used more often in order to get his habits under control. Most puppies will simply need a training refresher course so that they know what they are doing is wrong.

Remember, you should be the leader of the pack, not your dog. By establishing your role as the head of the household, this will give your dog some structure to how he should be acting. Know that any type of aggression should be taken very seriously because it can pose a threat to other dogs and even other people. This feeling is in your dog's nature most of the time. He isn't just going to run around biting people without any reason behind it. A timid dog might feel insecure and will rely on biting as a warning to stay away. A dog who is overly confident might also rely on this same behavior. Changing the habit comes from changing the balance of energy. No matter what is going on, your dog needs to know that you are the boss.

If you feel that you just cannot handle this behavior, it might be wise to look into some training classes. These classes are not meant to be a punishment; they are actually meant to be helpful to your dog. This is also a chance for him to get used to being around others in a passive way. The trainer will be able to provide you with tips on how to deal with aggression once you get home, too. In the meantime, learn what triggers your dog and keep him clear of situations like this. Big crowds or loud noises can often cause a dog to feel insecure, so if you can help it, keep the environment controlled. If you do have to go out in public, always keep your dog on a leash so that you can step in if you need to. Allowing him to get the experience of being in a public setting while still on a leash is a happy medium.

6

TOP MISTAKES MADE BY HUNTING DOG OWNERS

Getting a dog comes with a lot of trial and error. That is what Angela Hart thought when she finally got through with training her hunting dog, Lucky. She was under the impression that the training would be a breeze, simply following steps out of a book. What she actually ended up learning is that Lucky gave her a run for her money. A Pointer, Lucky did not come from a pair of hunting dogs. Instead, she came from the shelter. Wanting to do a good deed, Angela adopted her with the intent of grooming her into being the best bird dog in the South. Upon bringing Lucky home, Anglea realized that she was going to have to work pretty hard to accomplish this goal—Lucky chewed up her entire living room furniture set.

Once they got past this setback, Angela thought surely that Lucky would be ready for training now. She was doing a lot better with her temperament, and she even came out to the field a few times, displaying her eager obedience. It was their first hunt, and Angela had a lot of faith in Lucky. A group of birds were nearby, and before Angela knew it,

Lucky had taken off on her own accord. The birds scattered and Lucky continued running after them until she got tired, much to Angela's dismay. Surely, she thought, this wasn't going to work out. Her plan was to get another dog, keep Lucky at home with the kids.

There was a longing in Lucky's eyes a few weeks later. Angela had still not gotten another dog, but Lucky was kept at home for the most part now. She noticed that Lucky kept fetching a decoy and bringing it to her, tail wagging eagerly. With a sudden change of heart, Angela knew that she couldn't just give up. The pair worked tirelessly for a solid month, drilling these training exercises until Angela had confidence in Lucky again. It was time for redemption; they set out on another hunt. Admittedly still a bit nervous, Angela told Lucky to stay as they approached a huge flock. Still excited as ever, this time she stayed. It was a satisfying moment that showed Angela the value in trusting her hunting dog.

What Not to Do

It can be hard to have trust in your dog, especially when you are still in the early training stage. This is something that is essential to building a strong relationship, though. The mutual trust is what gets you from point A to point B. Making mistakes is to be expected, but if you are able to stop them before they happen, this will make your hunting dog training a lot easier. Here are a few of the most common ways that gun dog owners have admittedly messed up:

- Overdoing It: While it can be great to continue drilling the necessary skills with your dog, there comes a point when it all becomes too much. Knowing how to stop before your dog gets overwhelmed can save you from plenty of setbacks. Make sure that you are distributing an equal amount of time in basic training, field training, and at-home training. All three of these components make for a great gun dog, not just an abundance of one. If you feel that your dog isn't being responsive to the training after you have been going at it for some time, you need to give him a break. Imagine working your entire shift without the ability to step out and take a break. This is work for your dog, and you need to make sure that you acknowledge that.

- Losing Your Dominance: It can be hard to establish a sense of dominance, especially when you have such a sweet-natured pup. It is absolutely necessary, though. If you never establish this in the beginning, you cannot expect your dog to obey you once you bring him out into the field. Let your dog know that you have the ability to bring him not only positive reinforcement but also punishment when necessary. He needs to be able to feel that you are the only one who gets to make decisions when it comes to obedience. If you give him options, he will definitely become wilder as it is in his nature. Your dog should have no say in his gun dog training. While you definitely do want to treat him well, you also need to make it clear that you are the one giving the commands.

- Playing Tug-of-War: Any dog that you intend on making a hunting dog should avoid this game. This can actually cause your dog to unintentionally learn bad habits. While the tug-

of-war is fine for most dogs to play, gun dogs
must know that they need to give up the item
once they have it in their possession. The point of
tug-of-war is to not let go, even when the owner
insists. This will send a very confusing message
to your dog if he grows up playing this game and
then is suddenly being punished in the field for
not dropping the kill that it retrieves. Stick to
games that are more focused on fetching, speed,
and agility.

- Punishment for Retrieving: Even if your dog
  retrieves an item that you did not ask him to,
  steer clear of any form of punishment. This will
  confuse him when you are training him how to
  hunt. Instead, simply take the item away and try
  to put it where he cannot pick it up again. Dogs
  are going to be eager to please. If you do not offer
  praise and attention, it is unlikely that your dog
  will get a satisfactory response from retrieving
  the item. This is how you will teach him what
  you actually want him to retrieve, instead of him
  assuming that he should be picking up
  everything that he can.

- Changing Commands: When you pick a training
  command, make sure that you stick to it. For
  example, when you want your dog to come to
  you, make sure that you are utilizing only one
  command. While "here" and "come" can signal
  your dog to do the same thing, it is going to be
  much easier for him to follow your instructions
  when you pick just one command to use. The
  easiest thing to do is to write all of your
  commands down as you train. This will keep you

on track and it will also serve as a guideline for
what your dog should be doing.

- Children for Discipline: While integrating your
  gun dog into your child's life is a great thing, your
  child should never be the one doing the training.
  Remember, obedience has everything to do with
  dominance. When a child starts to order a dog
  around, this sends out a mixed signal. The dog
  will either challenge the command or begin to
  listen selectively. Either way, you want to keep the
  message very clear -- you are the one who gives
  the commands. Appropriate ways for your child
  to help come in the form of socialization and
  playtime. Absolutely allow your pup to interact
  with your child, given that he is of a good nature.
- Entering a Rut: The first few months after
  training at home and then heading out into the
  field can sometimes result in a training delay. You
  will want to make sure that the training never
  actually ends, even during times when you feel
  that your dog is on top of the latest commands.
  Even if you are just reviewing older material, it is
  important to keep running the drills that you
  have created. Dogs get bored easily, so if it feels
  like it is becoming redundant, change up the
  setting. You can train at home, in the field, or
  even at a local park. This simple change in
  scenery can have a great impact on your dog's
  ability to learn how to focus.

Consistency
One of the main take-away points here is that you must

remain consistent in everything that you do when you are training your hunting dog. From your commands to your drills, slipping up is bound to happen sometimes, but you should be making an effort to create a seamless training plan. Dogs will lose interest quickly, so it is important that you do have some variations of the same exercises. The consistency comes in with the goal that you are trying to achieve and the command that you are using to get there. As mentioned, writing down a list of all the commands that you want to use with your dog can prove to be very helpful. It will keep you on track as you train, and you will be able to have a concept of how well your dog is doing at mastering each one.

Tracking your training sessions isn't a bad idea, either. Using a notebook, you can log when you train, where you train, and how long you train. Make little notes that you will find useful for the next training session. In the notes, you might want to include things like: how focused your dog was, how many times he performed the action, and what skills that he needs to work on. This can also be a great way to let your trainer know what type of progress you have made (if you decide to utilize outside training resources). Remember, hunting is going to be equivalent to a job for your pup. Go ahead and make a training schedule that you can both stick to. It will make sure that you stay committed and consistent.

Select a few things each day that are not training related but are still going to form consistency. For example, maybe you can always take your dog for a 6PM walk. It could even be something as simple as sitting, shaking, and laying down before you feed him. The more consistency that you build in his daily life, the more comfortable he will feel with consistent training. As much as dogs like to have fun and unleash their energy, they do appreciate a sense of security just like people do. When confronted with a challenging situation, your dog will have more energy to put toward it because he will be comfortable in his everyday environment.

Make sure that the entire household is on the same page. While you are teaching your dog consistency, you won't want someone else in the house to be ignoring all of the rules. This is yet another way to confuse your dog and likely cause him to disobey your commands. Consistency needs to happen with everybody that lives in the house. Make sure that no one is rewarding him for behavior that he should not be rewarded for. The same can be said for people who visit your house. If your dog is not supposed to jump up on people, tell your guests not to praise this type of behavior. Little efforts like this will help your dog out in the long run.

Dogs are not able to generalize. When you teach a command in a certain room, moving into a different room might throw your dog off. This is why it is important to always drill your commands in several different environments. Your dog is not going to assume that sitting inside is equivalent to sitting outside. It is up to you to teach him this message. The very best way to accomplish this is through consistency. Even when it seems like your dog has the skill down, it is never a bad idea to check in and have a little training session to refresh his memory. Think of it like a surprise pop quiz that you are giving to your dog.

Know that you are going to have to repeat things over and over again—this comes with training any dog. Consistency in your mood and your tone must also be kept. If you are feeling tired or frustrated, your dog will be able to sense this. Make sure that you are entering each training session with a blank slate. Keep the mood upbeat unless you need to punish your dog for acting out. When it all starts to come together, you will see that all of your efforts have been worth something. Seeing the end result can be difficult, especially when you are training a puppy for the first time. It can be the most challenging, yet rewarding, experience.

7

HOW TO BEFRIEND A HUNTING DOG

E ric Ross set out on a hunt in early September of last year. He was excited to bring along Buster, the retriever. The pair trekked on for miles, unable to spot any animals, but still having a great time together. It was one of Buster's first big hunts, an overnight trip for the two of them. The plan was to hunt until sunset and then set up camp nearby. It was getting dark, so Eric figured that he would call it a day on this quiet hunt. Suddenly, he lost his footing as he was about to get up to find a place to set up camp. A hole swallowed his left foot, causing him to twist his ankle pretty severely. Unable to move and now suffering from a broken ankle, Eric slumped down onto the ground while Buster waited eagerly for him to get up.

Realizing that something was wrong, Buster ran over to him and began licking his face. He wanted to make sure that Eric stayed conscious through all of the pain that he was experiencing. Pulling out his phone, Eric called for help while Buster never left his side. Once the ambulance arrived, they found a sight that they would never forget— was lying beside Eric, occasionally licking his face and checking on him to make sure that he had not passed out. It was then that it was made certain, Buster was so much more than a hunting dog. He was Eric's best friend.

The Fine Line

As a dog owner, you often have to play multiple roles. You must make sure that your dog is happy and well cared for, but you are also the one who is responsible for his obedience and training. This is especially true when you are training a hunting dog. It takes a lot of effort in order to get your dog to do exactly what you need him to do when you are out on a hunt. How can you make sure that you are being good to your dog while also feeling like you are being a great trainer?

Bonding is one of the best ways for you to befriend your dog. It might sound like a funny concept, but you do need to win your dog over if he is going to have trust in you. Bonding can look like anything from a walk to a trip in the car together. It is an amount of time that is spent together solely for that purpose. When you are not training or playing, you should be doing things together that will allow your dog to get to know you. Just as your dog has a certain temperament with unique habits, so do you as a dog owner. Know that a mutual bond of trust is going to improve your relationship with your gun dog.

Before you think about hiring someone to sit with your dog or walk him while you are gone, consider bringing him along. Owning a gun dog is a commitment, one that you should only take on if you truly feel that it is going to fit within your current lifestyle. Dogs are similar to children in that they crave your attention. When you get off work, even if you are exhausted, take some time to pay attention to your dog. Even a brief acknowledgment can make your dog feel like a priority in your life. Thinking about things in perspective, we all have responsibilities that we must continually be aware of. To a dog, his only responsibility is to please his owner. Because you make up such a large part of his life, he might become very sensitive if you do not pay him enough attention.

Know when it is time to turn off your training voice and to just be yourself. Being genuine with your dog is the easiest way to begin bonding. This can start from the very beginning--when you two aren't working together, just be yourself. He will start to learn what your personality is like and vice versa. Dogs bond to their owners very quickly if given the chance. Know that any change or disruption in schedule can throw your dog off. If you suddenly need to work for an extra hour each night, do your best to fit in some additional bonding time with your furry friend. He will, definitely, appreciate it.

Taking Trips

Bringing your dog along with you to different places will provide him with a sense of importance. A trip does not have to equal a vacation; it can be as simple as having your dog ride along with you to the grocery store. When you do decide to take your dog on a trip, make sure that he is fully comfortable with being in the car. A dog who is nervous might start to act out while you are driving, which can be very dangerous. Do a couple of test drives around the block to see how your dog handles the motion. Some dogs love going for rides but end up getting carsick. Monitor his behavior and then use your best judgment for when you think you can take a longer trip. As mentioned, even a quick drive to the store can create a great bonding experience.

Depending on the type of car that you drive and your dog's temperament, you might want to consider getting him a seatbelt that will hold him in place. Some dogs do very well simply sitting in the passenger seat or backseat. If you notice that your dog becomes too hyper in the car for you to safely drive, your local pet store will sell dog seat belts. These devices clip into your normal seat belt buckle on one end and to the dog's harness or collar on the other end. It is like putting your dog on a short leash while riding in the car but in a safe way. Using an actual leash for this is hazardous because your dog can get caught by the leash if it has too much slack in it.

Try not to let your dog eat right before you get into the car. This will prevent him from getting carsick during the ride. Also make sure that you do not feed your dog immediately after finishing the ride. He will need time to adjust both being in the car as well as being back out of the car. To a dog, this change can feel a lot more intense than it does to humans. Feeding your dog a treat after the ride is a good way for you to show your appreciation of his behavior. This along with some praise will have your dog feeling comfortable and ready to ride anywhere. Getting in the car should be a fun experience, not one that he only associates with him being taken to the vet or groomer.

If you plan on being gone for an extended period of time, make sure that you bring along a bowl and some water that you can give to your dog. They can get very easily dehydrated while riding along with you. Most people like to keep a portable dog bowl in the car at all times just in case they need to provide their dog with some water. Once your dog starts riding with you more, you can start to do the same. Remember to never leave your dog in a hot vehicle for extended periods of time. The temperature can climb very quickly, and a non-ventilated space can be fatal to a dog that is left behind. Either take your dog out of the car or leave your dog at home if he cannot go inside the place with you.

Being Understanding

It can be hard to shake the disciplinary role, especially when the two of you have been training regularly for the hunt. While you always want your dog to be on his best behavior, both in the field and in the home, you do not have to approach each situation with seriousness. Be understanding of your dog when he is "off duty." Outside of your training sessions, you will still want to maintain a basic level of manners and behavior but understand that a dog is a dog. He might try to get playful and he might whine in order to get your attention. Simply turning to punishment right away is going to make your dog fearful of you. While do you want him to obey you, this does not mean that he has to perform the actions based out of fear. This is a common mistake that most hunting dog owners do not even realize that they are making.

As long as you are reasonable with your requests, your dog will pick up on the behaviors that you are trying to teach him. Having a hunting dog is all about balance. You need to maintain his skill level, but you also need to ensure that he feels happy and safe. When you are bonding with your dog, solely for the purpose of getting to know one another, try to soften your tone. Make sure that you use a gentle voice so that your dog knows that he can relax. Getting your dog to drop his guard around you is important. It is one of the highest forms of trust that you can experience with a dog. When he is able to show you his serious working side as well as his calm and relaxed side, then you know that you have a great balance of training and bonding.

Know that your dog is going to be more prone to acting out when you two are bonding. While it is important to curb this behavior, do it gently. By letting his guard down, he is showing you that he trusts you. This might cause him to become playful or even mischievous with his behavior. This is often when big dogs can revert back into acting like puppies. Most hunters will agree that they not only appreciate their dog as a hunting partner but also as a loyal companion. Some hunters do not think beyond the purpose of hunting for their dog. They are surprised to realize that they were able to form such a strong bond with the dog, so the saying still remains true—the dog is man's best friend.

Becoming Even Closer

If you feel that you already have a great bond with your dog but wish to make it stronger, there are still things that you can do in order to strengthen this bond. If you want to know how to get closer to your pup, try one of the following methods:

- Get on the Floor: Dogs love it when you put yourself on their level. By getting on the floor, you are showing him a form of affection. This action does increase your dog's power, so make sure that no rough housing occurs. Simply hanging out together on the floor is a great way to make your bond even closer. You can still maintain your dominance, as long as your dog is not allowed to jump all over you once you bring yourself down to his level.

- Participate in an Agility Course: This is a whole lot of fun combined with a test of skills. If you dog is active, he will likely enjoy trying out an agility course. During these tasks, your dog is relying on you to tell him what to do next. As you work together to complete the course, you are working on your bond. This can be a whole lot of fun for both you and your dog.

- Play Hide-and-Seek: Have you ever wondered if your dog's sense of smell was above average? Try playing a game of hide-and-seek in your house or yard. By hiding, you are giving your dog incentive to look for you. Any dog that loves his owner won't stop until he finds him. Once he finally sniffs you out, the result will be priceless. Dogs love it when they are able to find you after not being able to see you for a long time. Test your dog and see how long it takes for him to sniff you out.

- Be Affectionate: If you want to kiss your dog, do it! Much like humans, dogs tend to appreciate many forms of affection. They will understand what a kiss is, and it is likely that they will lick you back to show respect. When your dog licks you directly on the nose, this is one of the highest forms of respect that he can show. This means that he trusts you and knows that you are the boss.

8

HUNTING DOG SOCIALIZATION

A shy hunting dog? Surely, there is no such thing. This is what Benjamin thought when he brought his dog around others for the first time. It was a warm day at the park, perfectly sunny with just the right amount of wind chill in the air. Sonny was unsure the moment that his feet touched the grass. Ordinarily, he loved running around in big open spaces. He found himself a little bit insecure in the presence of all the other dogs that were playing at the park. Benjamin was confused. How was Sonny so sociable when they were together, but so shy when he was in the presence of others?

Thinking back to when Benjamin first brought Sonny home, he realized that he probably should have been more proactive when it came down to socialization. Sonny was an active pup, chewing up everything in sight at first. For this reason, Benjamin had to keep him in his crate for most of the day until he was able to fully supervise him after work. Sonny never really went to the park, and this explained a lot about his present-day behavior. Chuckling and shaking his head, Benjamin clipped the leash back on and headed home. In time, he realized that Sonny preferred one-on-one time with other dogs, as it was way less overwhelming.

Appointments

One of the very first places that you will likely take your pup is the vet's office. Because a dog needs to have proper immunization before he can interact with other dogs, being at the vet is one of the first situations where your dog is going to be socialized. This is both a blessing and a curse. While your dog is able to experience going out in public, the setting at the vet can be pretty scary. In order to avoid forming any type of negative association with getting in the car and going somewhere, try to praise your dog and get him excited. Make sure that you bring along treats and toys so that he will feel that this is a fun thing that he gets to do. Dogs can sense when their owners are nervous, so your nervous energy definitely does have the ability to affect him.

At the vet's office, you are likely to encounter other dogs and several other people. In order to keep a friendly pup, let him say hi to everyone that wants to say hi to him. When you get taken into the back, greet the vet like an old friend. This will establish that your dog can let his guard down, that he is safe. Because the situation will be new to him, you need to set the right tone. By establishing a great relationship with your vet, you won't have any problems in the future when it comes time for the annual checkup. Let your dog sniff around the room so that he feels comfortable. There are normally treats on the counter that you can give him, so make sure that you look for those.

While a trip to the vet isn't the most fun social event, it still counts as one. Getting your dog used to this type of setting can be just as important as getting him used to being in open spaces outdoors. Once you have mastered the vet visit, the next public place you will likely take your dog is to the groomer. This is another situation that might appear scary to a dog because of all the poking and prodding. You can use the same tactics that you did pre-vet—plenty of praise and treats. Get your dog in a great mood so that he will be comfortable and open to the experience. The same way that you greeted the vet, greet the groomer in a friendly way. This will establish a sense of security from the beginning.

It is good to expose your pup to these kinds of settings early on, especially if you intend on training him to hunt. Most people focus so much on getting the dog comfortable outside that they forget to socialize him in public. Being used to both of these settings will make for an all-around social dog. Ideally, you should be able to get your dog in the car, and he should be happy to ride anywhere. If he does get really nervous before going to the vet or groomers, you can try some holistic approaches. Adding a lavender supplement in his water can help with anxiety. There are also shirts that are called "thunder shirts" which wrap tightly around the dog's body to make him feel secure. Getting your dog comfortable is the best way to get him social.

The Park

Probably the most common way to socialize your pup, a visit to the park can be a lot of fun. When he is ready for his first visit, you can tell him where you are going and place some excitement on the location. It would be best to bring a ball or some kind of toy that he can play with. Some dogs don't take to others right away but playing in a public park can still feel just as exciting. Let him sniff around on his leash first, checking out the surroundings with you right next to him. This is when you'll use your best judgment. If he seems timid, you can take him to a quiet area and play fetch together for a little while. See how he reacts if other dogs come up to play, keeping the leash close by just in case. If you can tell that he is eager to run around, let him off the leash. Most dogs will take off running out of instinct but don't worry, his obedience training will bring him back to you.

The most important thing for an owner to do at a park is to just pay attention. A lot of people get into altercations when their dogs start fighting, but nobody was paying enough attention. If you see that your dog is getting picked on, try to get him out of the situation. Call him over to you and see if the other dog's owner is getting involved. In cases like these, you might just need to move away from the one who is causing trouble depending on how involved the other owner is. If you find that your dog is the one playing too rough, stop the behavior right away. A light scolding will be enough to convey your message. If he keeps acting out, calmly clip his leash back on and take him home. Let him know that he won't be allowed to play in the park if he acts out.

If the behavior continues each time that you bring him to the park, you might need to do some more at-home training before he can be allowed back. This type of behavior as a puppy can lead to bad aggression as a mature dog. Trying to avoid this at all costs, make sure that your dog has a clear understanding of obedience. Telling him to stop something should result in him immediately listening to you the first time. If you can, ask some friends to bring their dogs over so that they can socialize in your yard. This is going to be like a precursor to a park visit. Keep in mind that your dog might get territorial since the playtime is occurring in his own living space. You will need to monitor the pups the same way you would at the park.

Once he is ready, you can return to the park. A dog will

normally outgrow his defiant puppy behavior once you scold him a few times. Just make sure that you are keeping a close eye on him and his surroundings. Not only is this a great place for your dog to make friends, but it can be a way for you to network. If you notice that your dog takes to another particular dog, you can try to get the owner's contact information so that the dogs can play again. You'll come to find that socializing your pup is a lot like socializing a child. Your goal is to integrate your dog into every aspect of your daily life so that he will get used to his surroundings.

Aggressive behavior can put a huge damper on visits to a dog park. If you can't even get your dog into the park without him barking at other dogs, you will need to work slowly on this process. You can start by bringing your dog to the park, but not going within the fenced area. Walk him up to the boundary of the fence and see how he does. If he starts barking and acting aggressive, take him away and properly scold him. When he learns that this behavior will result in you two leaving the park, he will be receiving the message loud and clear. Eventually, you should be able to stand on the outside of the fence with your dog only displaying excitement to go play. Of course, every dog is different, so you will have to learn your own dog's unique temperament.

To reinforce your dog's positive behavior, you can allow him to have a treat each time another dog comes up to him and he does not bark. Each time that he acts aggressively, you can slowly begin to move back. For every good action, he will get to move forward. This is a very direct way to train your dog that his actions will impact the outcome. If you get to the point where you have taken several steps back, then you know that it is time to leave. Do not get discouraged;

your dog will have the ability to get over his aggressive behavior. Some just take more time than others.

Training Classes

If you find that at-home training just isn't enough, you can sign your dog up for some obedience courses. Most pet stores offer them, ranging from different ages to breeds. If your dog is especially aggressive or unruly, you might need to start off with some private lessons until he is able to work in a group. Not only will this improve your dog's behavior, but it will also give him the opportunity to meet other dogs during the classes. By placing him in a more formal environment, he will be likely to respond better to commands. Most dogs only need to take a few of these classes before the owner can tell a difference in the behavior. Know that enrolling your dog in a class does not mean that you've failed at training; he just might require a little bit of extra help.

Keep in mind that these classes can be a bit pricey. This is another reason why an owner might simply opt for an at-home training routine. If you are unsure about what the best decision is for your pup, ask the training school if you can try a drop-in class to see how your dog likes it. Based on demeanor alone, your dog might be better suited for doing the training in a less formal way. After one lesson, the trainer will be able to provide you with behavioral recommendations and a report of your dog's progress.

A lot of classes allow the owner to sit in which can create a strong bond between you and your pup. Taking these classes can provide your dog with stimulation that you might not be able to recreate organically. Because it is structured in a particular way, your dog's only responsibility in the moment is to learn the material. Think of it like school. As you see your dog work through the tasks, you might be able to have a better understanding of where he is coming from behaviorally.

Playdates

Probably the most fun for your dog of all the different methods of socialization, having a playdate is the ultimate reward. Meeting someone with a dog that your own dog gets along with is a treasure. When you first try to arrange the playdate, location is going to be important. Even the most well-behaved dog can get a little bit territorial. If you are having someone over to your house, make sure that you let the dogs first smell one another outside of the home. This will lessen the odds of a fight breaking out. Your home is also your dog's home, so he is naturally going to be very protective over it. Once they have been reintroduced and you feel that things are going well, you can take them off leash.

Running around in the yard and playing with toys is a great way to not only get their energy out, but to also work together. If you have friends that are also hunters, getting two hunting dogs together can be a great thing to do. Because both dogs will have similar obedience skills and training expectancies, they will likely get along well. You can even train them together, doing simple drills in the yard with decoys. When a dog sees another doing a task, it makes it seem even more appealing. This is a great trick to jump-start productivity.

If the dogs continue to play well together, you might even be able to take them both on a group hunt. This is something that is fun for the hunters as well as the dogs. It also provides you with an increased chance to find and retrieve prey. A little competition is healthy for your dog. It will show him that he needs to act quickly if he wants to be able to complete the tasks that you expect of him. Brain stimulation will also be increased because now he has to be aware of the other hunters in the group, as well as the other dogs. This is something that you might have to work up to, but it can be a very rewarding and sociable experience for your pup.

9

WHEN TO RETIRE YOUR DOG

It is a decision that no one wants to make, but how old is too old to hunt? This is the struggle that avid hunter Jason Moreno had to face when his trusted Lab began to slow down. After years of hunting in Wyoming, Jason knew that Lucas was starting to become weaker. He just didn't have the same energy levels as before, often wanting to lay down in the middle of the field and just bask in the sunshine. Instead of trying to push Lucas to his limits, Jason knew what he had to do. It was Summertime when Lucas was finally able to retire, but his retirement didn't mean that his owner was going to spend less time with him. It actually meant the opposite.

The pair were inseparable because Lucas came into the family when he was only 8 weeks old. Every trip to the grocery store, park, and more, Lucas still rode along in the passenger seat. This made it clear to him that he was still an important part of the family. It was only during hunting time that Jason left Lucas behind. Feeling guilty at first, he knew that this was best when he saw him curled up comfortably at the foot of the bed. The 6 AM sun was shining, illuminating Lucas' now-greying face. Pulling out a small bone from the pantry, Jason left it near the food bowl for Lucas to find once he woke up. A bond that could never be weakened, he knew that this was what was best for his prized veteran hunter.

Your Dog's Health

It can be a very tough decision to put your dog into retirement. The thing about hunting dogs is that they will likely want to keep going until you change something. When considering his overall health, you need to make the best decision that is going to benefit him in the long run. Hunting and retrieving takes a lot of energy and stamina. Naturally, your dog is going to slow down over time. You might also be able to recognize this change in your hunting buddy when he starts to show less interest in hunting. Eager to please you, he might still run through the fields. However, if you ask him to retrieve a kill and he does not immediately go toward it, you might want to consider that it is time for retirement.

It is very important for you to continue with his regular vet visits. Senior dogs often encounter health problems, so it is better that you stay on top of his health than waiting to receive bad news. If you are unsure about when you should retire your dog, you can have a discussion with your vet about the decision. Considering the health and function of your dog's joints is essential. Older dogs might have trouble with this, much like people do. Also, a decline in eyesight is a common ailment. These things need to be taken into consideration because your dog relies on them in order to hunt with you. Having a vet verify your dog's condition is going to be a very helpful factor regarding your retirement decision.

If your dog has ever been injured before, you need to

keep in mind that recovery is going to be a lot harder for a senior dog. Even without injury, you are going to want to make sure that he does not become injured for the same reason. Hunting takes a lot of endurance and the ability to adjust to different environments and climates. If you notice that your dog is having some difficulty, you will likely need to do an evaluation of his health. The most important thing is your dog's comfort and functionality. As people need to slow down when they get older, dogs are the exact same way.

Breed Consideration

At 7-years-old, a dog is officially considered a senior. Not all breeds age the exact same way, though. This is something that must be kept in mind. Once your dog reaches this age bracket, this does not necessarily mean that his hunting career is going to be over. There are several other factors alongside this one that you should take into consideration. Doing some research on your dog's breed should give you some insight into how many years that he has left for hunting. Larger dogs such as Labs and Goldens have an average lifespan of about 11-12 years. Using this information, it makes sense that age 7 will be the year that your dog will likely start slowing down.

Smaller dogs tend to have longer lifespans (around 14-16 years). If you have a hunting dog that is on the smaller side, it isn't uncommon to go into retirement at around 10-years-old or older. Again, this can vary depending on preexisting health conditions or other injuries that have been sustained. Some dogs are more prone to hip and joint issues while others will be the first to lose their eyesight and hearing. The main thing to remember is that choosing retirement is a decision that is up to you to make. While statistics and vet visits can guide you, what it all comes down to is how your pup performs during the hunt. If you notice that he is no longer enjoying it the way that he used to, then this should be an indication of what you need to do next.

Hunting is something that should always be exciting and enjoyable for a dog. Some actually have it in their breeding to *need* to hunt. Just as natural instincts are going to tell a dog to retrieve a kill, they will also step in when it is time for a dog to slow down. Thinking about the way that dogs age, it is a much quicker process than the way that we do. You can multiply 7 years to your dog's current age to find out the age that his body is equivalent. If you have a 9-year-old Lab, for example, he is actually aging at the rate of a 63-year-old human.

Make it Positive

While it can be very hard to retire your hunting buddy, this does not have to be a sad occasion. Remember, your dog can easily sense the way that you are feeling. If you are worried about disappointing or replacing him, he is going to feel this. Think about his retirement in a positive manner, a period of time where he gets to live life comfortably and relaxed. This is your chance to spoil him and allow him to ease up on his hunting training that he has held onto for so many years. While the training is never going to leave his memory, you can show him that it is okay to rest and to feel at ease.

One of the hardest things about this transition is showing your dog that it is okay to relax. Certain sounds and sights might trigger him back into hunting mode. He will also likely run to the door when he sees you grabbing your gun and setting out for the field. These instincts probably won't be unlearned, but you can help make this transition easier by encouraging your dog to stay put. Let him know that he is not being punished, but actually rewarded because he gets to remain at home and at ease.

If you still need to supplement his hunting time with some decoy fetching in the backyard, you can go ahead and do this so that he can get the urge to hunt out of his system. As mentioned, this instinct is likely going to be within his breeding, and if you need to do this, it can be a great compromise. Reverting back to the training exercises that you taught him when he was younger can give him the same satisfaction as a real hunt. Make sure that you pay attention to his stamina and that you do not work him as hard as you once would.

The decision to retire your hunting dog will not only impact him, but it will also have an effect on you. Make sure that you are also preparing yourself for the transition. Again, this does not have to be a sad time for moving on. Appreciate all of the years that you have spent out hunting together. Remember, just because your dog is retired does not mean that he is actually going anywhere. The bond that you have created will still remain when you get home from your hunting trips.

How to Keep Him Healthy

For preventative purposes, it is absolutely okay to take certain measures in order to preserve your dog's health. If he is definitely slowing down, but not quite ready for retirement, you need to ensure that you are taking these steps:

- Weight Maintenance: Keeping your dog at a healthy weight is important for many different reasons. Older dogs store fat differently, and this can be a key factor to certain health issues down the road. Make sure that his diet includes enough protein. You might have to switch to a different food that is geared toward senior dogs. If you tend to give him a lot of table food, make sure that you aren't feeding him harmful things like fried foods and fatty foods. A lean dog is going to function a lot better while you are out in the field.

- Regular Exercise: Since his training has already been mastered by this point, you probably don't exercise your dog as much as you did when he was younger. Exercise is important for dogs, and this includes those who are aging. Make sure that he is getting some exercise outside of your hunting trips. If the only time that he gets his heart rate up is during a hunt, then he will be sure to strain himself and become drained a lot easier. Walks, hikes, and trips to the park make great forms of exercise for senior dogs.

- Health Supplements: If you haven't already, ask you vet if there are any supplements that you should be providing your dog with. Those who have weak hips and joints are normally able to take vitamins that are in liquid form. A small amount mixed in the water bowl is enough to give your dog the nutrition that he needs. There are supplements for a wide variety of ailments. Consider this when you talk to your vet next time. Much like people take daily vitamins, this can help keep your dog healthy too.

- Vet Visits: Keeping up with your dog's regular vet visits is essential, especially as your dog gets older. Even if everything seems well externally, your vet is going to be able to give you a more in-depth look at how your dog is doing. Plus, it is important that you keep up with his boosters for Rabies, Parvo, and more. Regular examinations can help prevent some problems before they start. You can also ask your vet for some flea and heartworm prevention methods, as your dog should be taking a regular preventative product for both.

By taking a look at your dog, you can get a basic idea of how healthy he is. His eyes should be clear and bright; any discoloration or glazed appearance can indicate that he might need more vitamins and supplements. His ears should be free of wax and rid of any type of smell. When a dog has a wet, cool nose, this is a good sign. It can be an indication that he is well-hydrated. His mouth health is also important. While his teeth might have build-up, his gums should remain firm and not inflamed. His coat should be shiny and thick with no patches of fur missing. All of these things can be examined in order to get a full picture of how your dog is doing.

10

DEALING WITH YOUR RETIRED DOG

The dynamic between a hunting dog and his owner is unmistakable. All of those early mornings and thrilling chases have the ability to bring a pair close together. When a dog becomes a hunting dog, he serves a pretty straightforward purpose. Even if he gets love from you at home, he is also a very integral part of your hunting experience from the moment that he first sets foot on the field. During your time hunting together, it is unlikely that you are thinking about the day that he isn't able to hunt anymore. It is a reality that will come, though. Dogs age and then they must slow down, just like people. After accepting this, you have to think about the next stage —what does this mean for your relationship with your furry friend?

Albert Ross didn't know what to do after Buck got diagnosed with hip dysplasia. The diagnosis prevented him from being able to hunt anymore. One day he was fine, retrieving kills with ease. The next, he was having a hard time running in the backyard. After a vet visit, they determined that it would be best for Buck to stop hunting immediately. He needed proper rehabilitation because he hurt the muscle. Albert knew that his hip dysplasia wasn't going away, even after the muscle healed. He was left with no hunting partner and a confusing transition phase. He had always loved Buck, but now he had to think of new things that they could do together. From car rides to sitting beside one another in front of the tv, they were able to fill their bond with new things to do that were low impact.

Keep the Same Schedule

Just because the hunting stops does not mean that everything else in your dog's life must stop. A lot of owners don't know what to do when they receive the news that their dog's hunting career has ended. Instead of changing the entire schedule, all you have to be conscious of is filling the space that hunting once took up. When you think about it this way, the task doesn't seem quite as daunting. Continue with the same meal times. Dogs are very sensitive to the times that you normally feed them. Changing this, even by a couple of hours, might result in your dog to become upset or confused. If his food schedule is still the same, this keeps a sense of normalcy present.

Depending on what you normally do during the day, your dog is either going to be at home until you finish up or go with you. If possible, it would be nice to add a little bit of time together during the day with your pup. By adding these small things to look forward to, it is going to be easier to replace the hunting trips that you once took together. As long as his health remains, take him on regular walks so that he can get his exercise in. You can opt for a simple walk around the block or even take him on a hike so that he can get out of the house. Remember, your dog spends a majority of the time at home, so getting him out can be a fun thing for him to do.

Inevitably, you are going to continue hunting. Because your dog is so used to going along with you, it is going to be tough to break his excitement the first few times. He will probably jump up and try to get into the car with you. Give him a lot of attention before you go and assure him that he is being a good dog by staying put. Eager to please, dogs get confused when you do not allow them to help in the ways that they used to. It might be a good idea to give him a special toy or treat to keep him occupied before you leave for your hunt. This will send the message that you are still happy with him, even if he needs to stay at home.

Aside from the basics that you normally encounter on a daily basis, think of your dog's retirement as a chance to do exactly what he wants to do. Let him play, rest, run, or eat if that is what he is able to do. The idea of retirement comes along with the idea that the structure can be broken a little bit. Hunting dogs undergo rigorous training and sometimes strict rules in order to shape them into what they need to be on the field. Now, you are able to let some of this go. While your dog is naturally going to behave in a certain demeanor, show him that he can ease up. His free time can now consist of activities that are purely fun, not work.

It doesn't take much to keep your dog happy, so make sure that you pay close attention to his mood after the first few weeks of retirement. If anything, he will probably express some confusion during times when he is supposed to be hunting, but this should be the worst of the transition. Remember to exercise a good amount of patience during this time. A change is always going to take some time to get used to. As long as you work together, your dog should be all set to have a great retirement.

Introducing a New Dog

If you do want to get another hunting dog, you should

not feel guilty. This is not going to be a replacement dog, and that is what you have to keep in mind. Many people worry that their dog is going to feel replaced, when in reality, this actually means that he is going to have company from now on. Introducing an older dog to a new dog can go a few different ways. If your dog is great with other dogs, then this should be a flawless transition. Sometimes, older dogs like to take on a caregiver role and baby a new dog. Alternatively, because an older dog is so set in his ways, he might become territorial when inviting a new dog into the space. Younger dogs also have much more energy, which can become bothersome to a dog who is already at the age of retirement.

The introduction should be done outdoors, in the yard if you are able to. Allow them to meet while they are both on leashes. The energy is probably going to be excited at first, and they will need some time to smell one another. If your dog starts to get grumpy, create some distance between them. Remember, even if your dog has always been great with other dogs, having someone new in his territory could cause him to feel threatened. After things calm down, you can let your dog off leash. Allow him to lead you back into the house; this will give him a sense of authority in the situation. He is going to take on the role of Alpha. With your new pup on a leash, go inside the house and allow him to sniff around. This will solidify the role that each dog is going to take on. After this process is complete, you should be able to take the new dog off the leash. Your retired guy is likely going to follow the pup around the house until he settles down. This is normal, and you can allow them to explore together.

When you get a new dog, you can think positively about this new addition. When your dog gets along with a younger pup, this can give him a sense of purpose to take care of someone new. Your dog already believes that he must care for you, so giving him someone else to care for can be a great way to occupy his time. When you first start taking the new dog out on hunts, see if one of your family members can take your older dog to the park or to some other fun place. When he knows that you are only taking the new dog into the car, he could start to feel jealous. As long as you supplement his time, it shouldn't be hard to keep him happy.

Low Impact Tasks

Hunting is something that once gave your dog a purpose. One of the biggest changes for your dog will be a lack of responsibility. This doesn't have to end with hunting, though. If you would like, you can give him other tasks to do that won't wear him out quite as much. This will allow him to feel useful while still keeping his health in mind. The best way to do this is to think of some mental tasks for your dog to solve. Start with some puzzle toys. Dogs love the act of figuring out a toy in order to get to the treat in the middle. These are for sale at nearly any pet shop and are relatively inexpensive. Not only is this a fun activity for your dog, but it is also a way to keep his brain engaged.

If your dog misses being around water, you can buy a small children's pool or sprinkler for him to play in. This is a great compromise because he will be able to splash around without over-exerting himself. While this isn't the exact same thing as swimming in a lake, it can make up for the feeling. This is an easy way to allow your dog some fun outside of the house where you don't even need to leave your yard. It can also be a fun way for you or other members of the family to get involved during playtime. Dogs enjoy when you do the same activities that they are doing. This is one of the reasons that hunting creates such a bond. You can achieve the feeling this way, minus the acts that are going to wear down his endurance.

Hide-and-Seek is an exciting game to play with your dog. You can play this indoors or outdoors, giving you the option to play at any time. Start by bringing your dog into a room. Show him one of his favorite treats and make him sit down. Once he gets the chance to smell it, walk out of the room and tell him to stay. After you hide the treat, you can come back and ask him to "seek." This is one of those games that never seems to get old. Your dog will love the search, and not to mention, the great reward at the end of it. This type of game keeps your dog's mind sharp. It incorporates a lot of skills that he had to use for hunting. Just because he is now retired does not mean that he still can't utilize all that he has been trained to do. The Hide-and-Seek game is a happy medium.

When your dog is feeling extra playful, try to engage him in a Tug-of-War battle. There are toys, or simple ropes, that you can use for this one. This is the type of game that is interesting enough to get your dog excited, but low impact enough for older dogs. As long as you are keeping these two things in mind, there are countless other games that you can play and create for your buddy. Having a retired hunting dog does not mean you have to make your dog sleep the day away. A hunting dog is always going to have that natural instinct to keep moving, to keep working. What matters in his later years is the balance that you must keep in order to have the healthiest dog that you can.

11

THE OLD AGE OF A HUNTING DOG

U nderstanding the way that a dog ages is important to being a great owner. Dr. Charles Williams thought that he was an expert on the topic given his field. He was surprised to realize that, for dogs, the experience can differ greatly. His hunting dog, Luna, always kept him company on the weekends. For years, they would set out on different duck hunts. Some were successful while others were simply spent creating memories. Luna was relentless while she was out in the field, never wanting to miss a thing. As she started to get older, Dr. Williams was in denial that she was indeed slowing down. At 7-years-old, he started to notice several changes in her behavior.

A healthy Spaniel, Luna never had any health problems until she reached the "Senior" bracket. Dr. Williams took her to the vet to find that she had joint problems along with difficulty maintaining her endurance. Nothing in particular happened; aging had simply set in. After taking her on a few more months post-visit, Dr. Williams knew that he had to acknowledge her age. She also didn't seem to enjoy being out in the field as much anymore. It was time to retire and settle into her remaining years gracefully. After doing some research, he was able to provide Luna with the most comfortable solution for her ailments.

How to Hunt with an Old Dog

If you want to continue hunting despite your dog's advanced age, you must make sure that you are being cautious. Sometimes dogs are still able to hunt well into their senior years, but some modifications do need to be made. For one, the amount of running is likely going to have to be cut back. Running around for a long time is no issue to a dog that is in his early years. In fact, he will probably run around until he gets exhausted enough to nap. An older dog still has the same desire on the inside, and this is why you must be careful. Your dog might not stop running until he has over-exerted himself. As long as you are monitoring his behavior, you can come to a conclusion when it is time to rest. Make him take breaks and ensure that he has plenty of water to replenish himself with.

The easiest way to get your dog to rest is to lead by example. This means that you will likely have to slow down the pace of your own hunt to accommodate your dog. If you are still alert and moving around, your dog is naturally going to want to mimic this behavior. The same concept can be applied in regards to swimming. While swimming is a great activity, it can cause your dog to become easily exhausted. If he keeps getting in and out of the water, this might prove to be too much for his health. Only allow him to go in when you have a kill for him to retrieve. By changing this habit, you are still letting him have the experience, but you are limiting it for his own safety.

If your dog is on tracking duty, keep him close by. Let him use his pointing skills and his other senses to let you know exactly where the prey is. When you allow him to run ahead of you, this is another way that he might quickly become tired. Bring plenty of treats to show him that he is still doing a great job even when he is staying close to you. Some dogs will likely be confused by this change during the hunt, but it is essential if you want to make the transition for one that he can participate in. Know that all of these modifications are being done in order to help your dog continue doing what he loves. While it won't always be possible to bring him along on the hunt, you can modify each one so that he can partici- pate for as long as possible,

Hunting with an older dog is almost like hunting with a puppy again. The main difference is that he will already have all of his training knowledge. As your dog ages, imagine that you must be as gentle as you used to be. This can include small details like helping him into and out of the car or reminding him to hydrate himself by giving him plenty of chances to stop and drink water. If he can only handle an hour or two at a time, let him have the experi- ence. Many owners are okay with having less time to hunt if it means that their dog can still use the skills that he has grown to know and love.

Training an Old Dog

Your hunting journey might begin with an old dog. While it is not as common, plenty of people decide to get a hunting dog that is already mature. The saying that you cannot teach an old dog new tricks is untrue. In fact, training an older dog to hunt can prove to be quickly rewarding since the dog will likely know most of the basic obedience concepts that he needs to know. Because he is no longer full of puppy energy, he will likely be well-behaved when you are out in the field. When it comes to the training routine that you decide to use with a mature dog, you will likely need to make some modifications.

- Consider Past Training: When you are working with an older hunting dog, you need to remember that he has likely experienced some training in the past. Whether he was trained incorrectly or correctly, you are going to need to work around the behaviors that he has already been taught as "right." Start your training process as you would for a brand, new pup. You might come to realize that your mature dog knows different commands or has slightly different ways of following them. One of the most important steps, in the beginning, is getting to know one another. Once you have a good grasp on this, the rest of your training should go smoothly.

- Train Different Commands: As you learn which commands your dog already knows, you need to select the ones that you are going to be using as you hunt. If you plan on changing any of these words on your dog, you need to exercise patience. Your dog might react hesitantly to these new commands if he is already used to different ones. It is possible to recondition him to respond to the new ones, though. Just as you would with a younger dog, write down all of the commands that you intend on using. Write down some notes next to each one on your dog's progress and responsiveness to each one. If possible, it would be helpful to ask any prior owners about what commands the dog has been taught so far.

- Slow it Down: With an older dog, there is no

need to rush into things. He is going to need time to get used to what you are asking him to do. You can use a dull pinch collar to start; this will provide you with a decent amount of control without making the process seem scary. Go through your list of commands and physically respond using the control you have over his leash. If he responds well to this over time, you can let him off the leash and run through the same commands. This will show him that your trust is building. He will want to reach the same way toward you.

- Conditioning Counts: A great strategy to approach your training is to let your dog out in the field. Allow him to hunt on his own, and when you are ready, snap on his chord and begin training mode again. This will teach him that a firm snap means that he needs to become focused. Going back and forth from hunting to training is great on a mature dog's brain. It can teach him how to be aware of his surroundings, which is important when you need him to act precisely on the hunt. Keep the in-field training sessions short, just long enough for him to go over a few drills. You can then allow him to be at ease again, hunting as he likes.

- Electric Training Collars: Many people view electric training collars in a negative light, but they can be extraordinarily helpful when you are dealing with a mature dog. The important thing to remember is that an electric collar isn't meant to be a torturous experience for your dog. You can even try it out for yourself so that you will know what he feels. The small, quick shocks are meant to keep him focused. Your goal is to cause a reaction. When you use the collar, know that you should only activate it when your dog starts to misbehave or fall out of his concentration. Using common sense, you will know when the time is right. This also does not have to be a permanent training tool. Your dog will likely learn very quickly when you use this type of method on him.

- Give Him Experience: One thing that you must make up for when it comes to older dogs is the experiences that he would have gotten as a puppy who went on hunts. Take him to several different types of terrains and climates. You don't even need to be hunting but allowing him to experience all of the local ones will give him important experiences. If possible, you can also introduce him to many different types of birds. Let him see exactly what it is that he is supposed to be after. Your mature dog will be eager to see this all and thankful that you are allowing him to experience it.

- Behavioral Issues: When your dog shows you that he has some behavioral issues, you need to pay attention to them. It is likely that these habits aren't going anywhere, as the dog is already mature. It is not something that you can passively sit back and wait to change. The instant that you notice these things, you need to come up with an effective strategy to train these behaviors out. Older dogs will commonly develop these issues, so it is not usually something that should cause you to be concerned. As long as you are keeping up with his regular vet visits and training schedules, you will be able to work through these things together as a team.

- Consider the Inevitable: As you work with your mature dog and begin to hunt, you should keep in mind that this is a temporary partnership. Whether your dog needs to retire or your dog passes away, knowing that this is a reality will help you. Beginning this process with a dog that has already lived through the majority of his life can be tough yet rewarding. Enjoy these moments that you have together and make the most out of them. Allowing your mature dog to become a hunter is a great way for him to experience more of the world in his final years.

The process of training your mature dog will bring you challenges that you would not ordinarily face while training a puppy. Of course, there are pros and cons for each scenario. Know that it is entirely possible for your mature dog to become a great hunter, assisting you and ensuring that you have the most fulfilling hunting experiences. Even if you adopt your dog straight from the shelter with no prior hunting training, as long as you are willing to come up with a plan, your dog should be able to master all of the skills that he will need to know.

12

WHAT TO DO IF YOUR DOG GETS PREGNANT

A reality that hunters who own female dogs might have to face, finding out that your hunting dog is pregnant can leave you with some decisions to make. This is the predicament that Roger Allen had to face when he found out that Lady was going to have puppies. Allowed to roam freely in the yard, Roger had no idea that Lady and the neighbor's dog ended up breeding. Filled with rolling hills and not a fence in sight, Roger never considered that lady might have to be kept away from his neighbor's dog. She was a great hunter, at it for almost 4 years. Getting pregnant changed the dynamic, and it led Roger to the decision that she needed to retire once she had her pups.

HIS DECISION CAME from the fact that it was prime hunting season, but Lady was going to be out of commission for a while, not only during her pregnancy but also in the weeks to follow as she cared for her litter of pups. This worked out well in his favor, though. After Lady gave birth to 5 healthy pups, she was spayed to prevent further pregnancies. A few months later, Roger began training one of the most eager pups to be his new hunting dog. The skills stayed in the family, and this was the official start of Lady's successful retirement.

KNOW the Signs

EVEN IF YOU do not believe that your dog has a chance of getting pregnant, you never know what might happen. When your dog isn't spayed, you need to pay close attention to her heat cycles. When she is in heat, this is going to attract the attention of any surrounding male dogs. Being aware of the signs of heat and pregnancy will keep you prepared for what might happen.

HEAT

TYPICALLY, a female dog will go into heat twice each year. This can start to happen when your pup is as young as 6-months-old. Each cycle lasts around 21-28 days, but this can vary depending on your dog. There are physical signs that can indicate that your dog is in heat. For example, her vulva might become slightly swollen; this is one of the easiest signs to spot right away. Discharge is also normal during this stage. Make sure that you pay attention to her urination schedule. A dog in heat is likely to need to urinate more frequently than a dog who is not.

. . .

THE SECOND STAGE of heat is the one that is most easily recognizable. Your dog will have bloody discharge, and this is an indication that she is ready for breeding. Most owners utilize diapers in order to keep the experience as clean as possible. You might also notice your dog moving her tail to the side, indicating that she is fertile and going through the natural behaviors that come along with her being in heat. Even through the final stage of heat, your dog is still likely to become pregnant. The discharge might stop, and her behavior will return to normal, but be aware that the risk is still present.

Pregnancy

A DOG'S pregnancy normally lasts for 2 months. Many things change in this short period of time that are clear indications of what is happening. Pay attention to your dog's weight if you feel that she might be pregnant. This is the most obvious of all the signs, but it is often overlooked if the owner is not expecting a pregnancy. Also, consider any changes in her appetite. A pregnant dog is going to eat more and have a noticeable spike in her appetite. Another physical indication of a pregnancy can come from an increase in the size of your dog's nipples. As the milk is forming in the ducts, this will cause the nipples to appear swollen and larger.

OF COURSE, the best way to determine if your dog is pregnant or not is by taking her to the vet for testing. There aren't any at-home kits that you can use like the ones that are available for people. Your vet is going to have the proper equipment to test your dog, as well as view the puppies by using ultrasound technology. During this appointment, if she is far enough along, you will likely be able to see how many puppies she is expected to have. While your dog might carry a lot of puppies, know that it is common for some of them to pass away during the delivery. This is something that is typical during dog pregnancies simply due to natural causes.

CARING for a Pregnant Dog

IF YOUR DOG BECOMES PREGNANT, regulating her diet is going to be one of the first steps to ensuring that she has a healthy pregnancy. During this time, you will want to opt for high quality dog food that contains plenty of protein. When she is in the beginning stages of pregnancy, it is unlikely that you will have to change anything (unless the vet recommends a change). As her weight increases, make sure that you are gradually increasing her food intake. On average, a dog will end up consuming 35-50% more food toward the end of her pregnancy. This normally happens during the last 5 weeks. You might have to change her feeding schedule during this time, as large meals can be upsetting to her stomach. Switch to smaller meals that occur more frequently throughout the day. You can add to the portion size slowly so that she does not have any trouble with digestion.

MUCH LIKE PEOPLE, dogs will also have to go to the vet for

frequent check-ups. These visits are meant to make sure that everything is going well during the pregnancy. Your vet will be able to examine the overall health of your dog and the condition of all the puppies, too. This is also a time when you can ask your vet about getting your dog spayed after the puppies are done nursing. Many owners opt for the surgery if their dog has gotten pregnant by accident. Discuss what you can do to help your dog have a successful labor and delivery. While there isn't much that you can actually do to help her during the process, you can know what to look for in case an emergency situation arises.

YOU WILL WANT to make sure that she has a comfortable space to deliver puppies. You can use a whelping box for this. They offer a safe space for your dog to give birth while also being convenient for you to check on her. You can either purchase one or make your own, a simple nesting box that will allow your dog room to lay down while keeping the puppies safely inside. If you plan on using one for the birth, allow your dog to become familiar with it beforehand. You can set it up and let her get inside of it prior to her labor so that she feels comfortable using it. Introducing the box too late might mean that your dog will not think of it as her own safe space. She might opt for a closet or other small room when it comes time to deliver.

THERE ARE some items that you should have on-hand to help assist with the delivery. Consider picking up the following items:

- Newspaper: You can line the whelping box with newspaper to make for an easy clean-up. Placing this underneath any towels or blankets that are used can ensure that the actual bottom of the box will stay clean.

- Thermometer: Your vet will be able to instruct you on what a normal temperature should be during the labor and delivery process. Having this handy will allow you to check on your dog and make sure that she isn't breaking out into a fever.

- Scissors and Dental Floss: These items are going to be helpful when it is time to cut the umbilical cords. Use the scissors to cut the cords and the floss to tie off each of them. This will make for the most sanitary way to keep them tied off.

- Heating Pad: After the puppies are born, it is important that you keep them warm. You can use a regular heating pad for this purpose. Try to find one that has different heat settings so that you can be sure the temperature stays just right for them. You will want to be careful of overheating them.

- Towels and Paper Towels: After the delivery, keep all of your towels near for cleaning purposes. Each pup will need to be cleaned off, and the surrounding area will also need a good cleaning. Once you have removed the newspaper from the whelping box, you can replace the towel so that they have a soft surface to rest on.

- Contact Information: If at any point you suspect that something isn't going well, keep your vet's phone number handy. Know the hours of operation and keep in mind where the closest emergency clinic is. While you aren't going to anticipate a vet visit during the birth, you never know what might happen. It is always better to be prepared.

WHEN IT COMES to what you can actually do for your dog during the delivery, you won't play a very large role. Dogs have a relatively easy time getting through it on their own. Being nearby and observing is probably the most involved thing that you can do in the moment. Your dog is naturally going to know what to do when the puppies are born, tearing through each placenta and cleaning each pup off. If you notice that a puppy has been enclosed in its placenta for more than a minute, then you can assist by taking him out of it. They can only survive a couple of minutes while in the placenta after they have been born. After the cleaning processes, your dog should naturally sever the umbilical cords. If she does not, then you can use the scissors to cut them yourself. Leave about 1-2 inches of space between the cord and the puppy if you decide to step in.

AFTER THIS, you can observe each of the pups to make sure that they are breathing normally. Remember that there is a chance for some to be stillborn. While complications aren't anticipated, it is smart for you to learn the signs of distress. Labor can take a long time, but if 2 hours go by in between the delivery of each pup, this could be an indication of a problem. Keep an eye on her contractions, too. Any contraction that lasts for longer than 45 minutes is also the indication of a possible problem. If this is happening without any puppies being delivered, there is a chance that your dog is in distress and a visit to the vet is necessary. The entire experience can seem scary, especially if this is your dog's first time being pregnant. Just know that your energy is going to impact your dog. Keeping calm and allowing the process to happen naturally is the best thing that you can do for her.

WHEN TO STOP HUNTING

FINDING out that your dog is pregnant means that you will have to make a decision—when is it time for her to stop hunting? Ultimately, your vet is going to be able to give you the best advice. Some hunters still bring their pregnant female dogs out until they get close to their delivery date. The subject is up for debate among the hunting community.

Observe your dog and do pay close attention to her if you still decide to bring her on hunts while she is carrying. You need to make sure that you aren't overworking her. This is going to be especially important to her having a successful pregnancy. If she experiences too much stress, the puppies are unlikely to make it or will be born with health problems. Again, your vet is going to be able to provide you with the best opinion on what you should do.

ANOTHER DECISION MUST BE MADE after she gives birth, and this involves either spaying her or letting her enter heat again. If you plan on breeding her again in the future, you will need to track her heat cycles so that you can be prepared. As a dog gets older and if you do not want to breed her, getting her spayed is going to be a great decision for the quality of her health. Going through pregnancy and experiencing heat can take a toll on your dog. After you get her spayed, she is going to need additional time out of the field in order for her incision to heal. You will need to do your research before making the decision to get her spayed. There are many benefits to getting her the procedure. It can prevent tumors from growing and uterine infections from occurring.

SPAYING your dog will allow her to live a longer and healthier life. If you never intend on breeding your dog, you should consider spaying her when she reaches the proper age. It is normal to consider spaying after she reaches 8 weeks of age. The surgery should happen before she enters heat so that her body won't have to endure the cycle. Spaying your dog can also lead to positive impacts on her behavioral traits. Dogs that aren't spayed can often display high levels of energy and can be hard to train. After the surgery, you will notice that she is a lot calmer and more willing to listen to you. Talk to your vet about your options and when you should proceed with it.

13

HOW TO GIVE YOUR BEST TO YOUR HUNTING DOG

Ol Red was only supposed to be a pointer, accompanying Paul on his weekend hunting trips. He started out as a hunting dog but ended up as so much more. The pair would train together during the week and then set out on their hunts, utilizing all of the skills that they worked on. Paul was super happy with Ol Red's progress and didn't imagine that their relationship could get any better. One day, Paul found himself with an injured foot and was forced to spend the weekend at home on the couch. Being partly immobilized, he was flipping through the TV channels and dreaming about the next time he would be able to get out of the house to go hunting. He imagined that Ol Red was probably wondering why they weren't out on the field, too.

He wasn't expecting it, but Ol Red came into the living room and stood in front of Paul who was reclined on the couch. "I'm sorry," Paul said to him. The dog looked at him for a moment before walking over to the couch and resting carefully beside Paul. His head was gently placed in his owner's lap and he sat there with patience that Paul had never known before in his life. This is how he realized that Ol Red was much more than just a hunting dog; he was a companion through and through. From that moment on, Paul knew that he wanted to give his dog the very best while he had him.

Commitment

Getting a hunting dog is a lot more than just having help while you are out in the field. It is a long-term commitment to an animal that is going to grow to love and care for you the same way that you will love and care for him. Before you proceed with adopting a dog, make sure that you know enough about each breed that you are considering. Keep in mind that some dogs work best with retrieving while others are great at pointing. You are going to need to have enough space in your home to accommodate your new pet, too. Big or small, having a yard is going to benefit your dog by proving him an area to play and learn in.

Most dogs are going to be with you for at least a decade, so you must keep this in mind. If you are considering moving in the future or making big changes, considering your dog is important. You must move into a place that can accommodate your dog and his needs. Getting a dog is almost like having a child. There are plenty of basic needs that must be covered in order for your dog to feel content. It would not be fair to bring a child into an unprepared household, so consider the same when you are ready to adopt a dog. You will need the right supplies and the time, energy, and effort behind his training.

Company

If you do not have enough time to spend with your dog, then you should consider getting your dog a companion. Having another dog in the house can help with issues of loneliness that might arise. When it comes to having another dog around, you do not necessarily need to get another hunting dog. When your dog isn't out in the field, any company at all will be appreciated. Most of the time, dogs prefer to be in packs. When you bring him home, you automatically become a part of his pack. Through the trust that is earned, you will eventually be acting as the alpha. If you work a job that limits your free time, then know that this is an option that you can pursue.

Of course, his temperament will have a lot to do with this decision. If your dog is naturally defensive, then he might not appreciate another dog in the house. You will have to test his behavior as he grows. Another option is getting a dog sitter during the days when you know you will be gone for long periods of time. Having a friend or family member over that you trust will also suffice for those longer days. There are plenty of options for you to keep your furry friend occupied, so make sure that you consider all of them.

Travel

Bringing your dog along with you to several different places will make his life fulfilling. A simple trip to the park can make his day when it might not be something that you actually think twice about. Consider that you are essentially responsible for the activities that your dog gets to do each day. While routine is relatively normal to an animal, changing it up can make all the difference. Make an effort to take small trips in the car with your dog. This will not only get him used to various travel situations, but it will also keep him excited and happy. It truly will not take much to please him.

Getting to explore is one of the biggest joys that your dog can experience. Try taking him to new parks or trails that he can sniff out and roam around. He will be working on his tracking and observational skills while also getting the chance to experience something new. If you cannot bring him to an outdoor location, try going over to someone else's house. This is going to provide the same feeling of excitement in a very simple way. He will be eager to look around and explore his new surroundings.

Hygiene

Much like you feel better when you have a long shower, your dog is also going to feel his best when he is clean. He is naturally going to clean himself to the best of his ability, but it is up to you to bathe him. Whether you decide to do this at home, outdoors, or at a grooming facility, this is essential for keeping him in his prime. Most dogs that hunt are going to be accepting of water, especially those that swim on a regular basis. A weekly bath will be refreshing enough to rejuvenate him, but also simple enough for you to keep up with. If he has a long coat, you will also need to consider getting haircuts. This can either be done from home or at the groomers, too.

If you keep him in a collar most of the time, it can feel nice to take this off at night. When he is sleeping or resting, the collar might become uncomfortable. The noise of his tags might also become disturbing. Consider what might prevent you from getting a good night's sleep; almost all of these things will also apply to your dog. Try to keep his sleeping space as quiet as possible and ensure that he gets plenty of rest before you go on your hunts. If he sleeps in a dog bed or on certain blankets, wash them frequently. Just as you wouldn't want to sleep on a dirty bed, your dog is also going to be more comfortable sleeping in a clean space.

Food

As you have learned, what your dog eats is very important to his health and ability to function. A dog that is doing plenty of physical activity is going to need a diet that consists of a lot of protein. There are certain dog foods that are appropriate for certain life stages. A puppy is going to need different food than a senior dog. If you are having trouble deciding what diet will work best for your pup, talk to your vet about your options. Store-bought foods come in either dry or wet varieties. They are popular and common amongst hunting dogs, but some owners do decide to feed their dogs "table foods." This means that the diet will consist of fresh foods that are prepared regularly by the owner.

Your dog is going to have preferences, just as you do. It might take some time to learn which foods he enjoys the most. Changing up his food can also make a difference in his overall happiness because the variety is usually appreciated. Having the same food for a long period of time can get very boring to a dog. He might actually refuse to eat it after a while. You can also try some quick fixes—like adding a bit of chicken stock into his regular kibble. This will add some additional flavor while also making the food seem like it is new.

Fun

While you likely know the most common ways to get a dog excited and active, here are some additional ways that you can bring some more fun into his life:

- Get a Baby Pool: A great way to play outdoors, this can be something that your dog can claim as his own. Baby pools are relatively inexpensive and don't take much time at all to fill up on a hot day. Your dog will love splashing around and playing with his toys in the shallow water. Giving him space to just be free and playful is important, especially when he is normally very focused and disciplined while you are out on a hunt.

- Let Him Destroy Toys: Get him toys that are going to be designated as ones that he can destroy. It is within his natural instinct to want to tear his toys apart, especially the ones that resemble animals. Giving him permission to do this to toys can prevent him from acting out in other ways. If you start doing this when your dog is a puppy, he will learn that this is a special activity that he gets to partake in.

- Make Treasure Hunts: You can do this easily by using toys or treats to entice your pup to play the game. A treasure hunt can be as simple as hiding some treats around the house for your dog to find, or as complex as creating an entire setup in your backyard. These type of activities are great for engaging your dog's brain while he is simultaneously having fun.

These are just a few of the ways that you can bring more fun into your dog's life. As you can see, they are very simple actions that can go a long way. Your dog is not very hard to please. As long as you express your excitement, his energy level is likely going to match up with yours. If you want to give him the best in life, all that really comes down to is giving him enough attention and care. Being a dog owner does not have to be difficult; it can actually prove to be a fun and rewarding experience for you as well.

14

A COMPREHENSIVE REVIEW

Putting everything that you have learned together, you are going to be able to raise your hunting dog to be the very best. Starting from the beginning, know that selecting the right breed is going to be a key step when you are trying to pick the perfect companion. Consider what type of hunting you are going to be doing and what you would like your dog to do for you. Most commonly, hunters like their dogs to point, retrieve, or do both. Some even like for their dogs to actually hunt on their own. No matter what it is that you plan on doing with your dog, you must make sure that you are selecting a capable breed.

Remember the size of the breed that you are considering, and if you have enough physical space to take in a dog of that size. When you aren't hunting, you need to make sure that your dog is going to be able to live comfortably in the household, too. While having a yard isn't a necessity, it does make a difference when you have some open space for your dog to run and roam. Naturally explorative, a hunting dog is going to want to go off on his own every now and then. If you do not have a yard, make sure that there is easy access to a park of some kind in your neighborhood.

Pay close attention to the health and demeanor of the puppy that you choose. You will also want to take his history into account. Remember, those that come from hunting parents are usually going to be the ones that grow into great hunting dogs themselves. These skills can often prove to be genetic. You are going to want a dog that is sociable, yet intelligent. He must have the capacity to complete many different tasks while also remaining loyal and obedient to you. This is a multi-faceted animal that you are going to be asking a lot from.

If you do not select a puppy, bringing home an older dog is also a valid option. Keep in mind that you will need to know about the dog's past in order to determine how easy he will be to train for hunting. Is it in his blood? Has he had basic obedience training in the past? What type of setting has he been living in? This will all play a part in his demeanor. Your connection to a mature dog is also going to be important. It might be harder to get close to him if he has been living with another family for some time already. Know that it is possible to train an older dog to hunt with you, though.

In the Beginning

After you bring your dog home, this is a period of time where you will get to know one another. Observe what he enjoys and what he does not enjoy. Try your best to spend as much time with him as you can in order for him to become comfortable with you. The faster that you are able to build your trust with one another, the easier the training process becomes. You are going to take on the alpha role, and you will want your new dog to know this right away. Letting him get away with too much, in the beginning, will only promote his resistance to your commands and other training.

Your basic level of training should include commands such as sit, stay, and come. Potty training is also done at this point, if you have selected a puppy. Dogs are normally very eager to learn these simple, yet useful, skills. Practice them often, even when you are not training for the hunt. These are going to form your dog's basic set of manners that he should remember both inside and outside of the house. You can choose to train him with only verbal commands, or you can utilize a clicker. Whichever method you select, make sure that you stay consistent with it so he can get used to it.

Introduce to him the difference between playtime and work time. Let him become more explorative and independent during the times that you are allowing him to play. Make sure that you are changing the tone of your voice when it is time to get into training mode. If he knows the difference early on, it will be easier to get him to behave in the way that you want him to. Now would also be the time to introduce him to a crate if you plan on crate training. Again, consistency is going to be the key factor here. Make sure that you use the crate all the time if you plan on training with it. Not only will it become a main element in your sessions, but it will also give your dog a safe space that is his own.

As He Grows

Your dog's body is going to be changing a lot within the first few months. Depending on the breed that you chose, he is likely going to drift through stages of feeling that his feet are too big for his body. Work around this as best as you can with plenty of patience. Much like people, dogs also will not realize what exactly is happening as they enter puberty. Allow your dog to meet other dogs once he has successfully received all of his required vaccinations. This is the time when you will get to gauge how he feels regarding socialization. Some owners will have work to do in this department, but others will find that their dogs handle socialization really well.

Closely monitor your dog when he is around other dogs. You will want to carefully read his body language to make sure that he is not feeling threatened or aggressive. A dog's temperament can change incredibly quickly and can be triggered by many different things. Do not become discouraged if he doesn't like other dogs at first. Sometimes, a dog can simply be shy and nervous that other dogs are going to dominate a situation. Try to give him as many opportunities as you can to interact with others, even if this just means taking a walk around your neighborhood.

Once he is a few months old, you can introduce the hunting commands that he will need to know when he is out in the field. The choice is yours when it comes to which ones he is going to learn. Think about the kind of actions that you are going to expect him to perform, and choose your commands based off of this. It makes sense to write down the commands that you pick for the sake of consistency and organization. Jotting down notes on your dog's progress with these commands can also prove to be helpful. You will be able to see a true progress report and know which things he responds best to.

This is also the time to introduce him to decoys and drills. Try to recreate a hunting experience as best as you can for your dog. Let him see, smell, and hear all of the guns that you plan on using. It is the time where you must make sure that you are doing your best to desensitize him so that he does not get scared when it is time to hunt. Let him see and swim in water. Cover all of the bases for all of the different activities that he is going to be expected to do. This is going to be a period of accelerated learning and true bonding. Your dog is really going to be getting comfortable with you during this time.

Field Work

It makes sense to bring your pup out to the field as soon as possible. He must be used to the different settings that he is going to be working in. Make sure that he understands exactly what it is that you are asking him to do. If you want him to be a retriever, you need to introduce him to a bird so that he knows what he is after. Surprisingly, one introduction might be all that it takes for your dog to pick up on what he is supposed to do. A lot of dogs, especially ones that are bred for hunting, have a natural instinct that tends to kick in. Make sure that you praise him efficiently when he is able to perform a task. Plenty of praise and treats are going to come in handy for this. Your dog should feel proud and excited each time that he does something right.

For a tracker, getting him used to a live scent is going to be an important step. This can be easy to accomplish with store-bought methods, but you can also simply let him roam the field until he comes across the prey on his own. As long as he has mastered his basic foundation of training, he should be ready for this type of task. When you need him to stay put or come back to you, it should be no problem. If you feel that he isn't listening as well when you are out in the field, you might need to revert back to your first few training exercises. Try doing them when you are in the field so that he knows he must obey both at home and out in the open.

Behavioral Problems

Even the best dogs can experience some bad behavior. This might not even be to any fault of your own; a dog can start feeling something that makes him want to resist training. In order to avoid this, you need to determine what is causing him to act out. Take a look at his surroundings and his habits. Think about anything that you might be able to change in order to make his life more comfortable. Does he feel threatened? Scared? Worried? This step of observation on your end should always occur before any type of punishment is given. If you simply resort to punishing your dog, he might become even more withdrawn from you. Remember, you are someone that he should be able to trust.

You might need to do some extra work in order to break your dog's bad habits. This concept is no more complex than any other training session. It simply requires you to be vigilant and observant. As long as you can see what the problem is, then there should be no problem coming to a solution. You'll notice that your dog is happier when he has a better set of habits. Dogs will naturally want to do what is "right" so that you will be pleased with them. This is why showing praise for good behavior is going to set him up on the right track.

Social Settings

In the same way that it is important for humans to socialize when they are young, dogs need to meet other dogs. You can do this in many different ways such as through a dog park or a friend who has a dog. When it comes to socialization, your hunting dog does not only need to interact with other hunting dogs. In fact, it would be much more beneficial for him to meet dogs that are of all different breeds, sizes, and ages. Let him play with other dogs on a regular basis. As long as the sessions are monitored, he is likely just going to do his own thing. This is where his true personality will be able to shine through.

Even simple things such as car rides into town and vet

appointments can be a chance for your dog to work on his socialization. Let him meet people, as well as other dogs. A hunting dog needs to be open for the unpredictable, in all kinds of settings. If he is skittish or untrusting, then your hunt is going to be a lot more difficult because you are going to pay more attention to him than to your hunt. Let him have plenty of experiences early on so that he will be used to them by the time he reaches adulthood.

The Final Years

During your time as a hunting dog owner, you are going to experience countless things together. Some will make you happy and proud, while others will leave you feeling frustrated and confused. No matter what you go through, the experience is yours to share. A bond with a dog is a bond like no other, and this is what you will soon discover. Your hunting dog becomes much more than a worker; he will ultimately become your most trustworthy companion. Treat him well and he will do the same to you. His career isn't going to be permanent, so when you do need to come to the point where you retire him, make sure that you substitute his time well. He will continue to want to do his best for you for the rest of his life.

CONCLUSION

Thank you so much for reading. If you liked it, please leave a review.

If you want more great information, sign up for my newsletter for weekly dog training tips!- https://bit.ly/2XM9gi2

Made in the USA
Middletown, DE
14 May 2021